CUTTING AND DRAPING

party and eveningwear

Pattern Cutting for Special Occasion Clothes

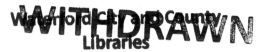

Dawn Cloake

BATSFORD

First published in the United Kingdom in 1998
by Batsford
1 Gower Street
London, WC1E 6HD

An imprint of Pavilion Books Company Ltd

This edition first published in the United
Kingdom in 2016.

ISBN: 9781849943710

A CIP catalogue record for this book is available
from the British Library.

20 19 18 17 16
10 9 8 7 6 5 4 3 2 1

Repro by Mission Productions, Hong Kong
Printed by 1010 Printing International Ltd, China

This book can be ordered direct from
the publisher at the website:
www.pavilionbooks.com, or try your
local bookshop.

Distributed in the United States and Canada by
Sterling Publishing Co., Inc. 1166 Avenue of the
Americas, 17th floor, New York, NY 10036, USA

Dress on cover form the autumn/winter 95/96
Tomasz Starzewski collection,
177–8 Sloane Street, London, SW1X 9QL.
Photographed by Timothy Griffiths.

Dedication

I dedicate this book to Dr Marysia Kratimenos
of the Royal London Homoeopathic Hospital,
Great Ormond Street, who, with Dr Peter Fisher
and the excellent staff of that great hospital,
made the completion of this book possible.

Acknowledgements

I would like to thank the staff of the DALI
(Developments at London Institute) Professional
Development Unit at London College of Fashion
for their continued support. To Alanah Cullen,
Business Manager, Catherine Fuller, Study
Abroad Director, Jane Cullen, Antoinette Oluwa
and Jyoti Shah, all of whom make teaching for
this institution a great pleasure.

My thanks are also due to Kennett and Lindsell
for the continued loan of the dress stand for
many of the diagrams in the draping section
of the book; to my business partner Susan
Chamberlain for opening up new horizons for
pattern cutting and sharing a new enterprise
with me.

Lastly, but most importantly, I thank my
husband for his unfailing support, advice and
encrouagement.

CONTENTS

INTRODUCTION

Cutting and Draping Party and Eveningwear concentrates on the construction of blocks and patterns for very close-fitting bodices and other dramatic style features found in evening and partywear. Instructions cover developing basic blocks into dress and jacket blocks and also into blocks for stretch fabrics; styles include strapless and draped bodices, low necklines, tight-fitting sleeves, fishtail skirts and godets, Princess- and Empire-line dresses, bustiers with and without sleeves, halter and cowl neck bodices, wrapover skirts and trousers with shaped and raised waistlines.

The book begins with a summary of dart manipulation, showing how to achieve curved and angled darts by the pivoting method, and follows with a section on blocks (basic patterns), explaining how and why these basic blocks and commercial pattern shells need to be adjusted for many special occasion clothing designs.

The book need not be worked through chronologically, but should be dipped in to for the answers to specific problems.

Where a number of similar garment designs may be required (for instance, when working in a design room) a good investment would be to make starter blocks for advanced styles for permanent use. Bypassing the basic block in this way avoids pattern cutting decisions and extra construction stages, allowing you to work faster and more efficiently. Strapless bodices need overall adjustment to achieve a close fit which will keep them in place during wear; low, wide necklines need tightening to prevent gaping; sleeveless styles need a tightened front armhole, even for low underarm styles, and stretch fabrics require block adjustment to reduce considerably (and sometimes eliminate altogether) the tolerance allowed in basic blocks for normal body movement. These adjustments, instead of being made individually for each separate design, need be done once only, the alterations marked on the new block, and the tightened shape recorded as a new secondary block specifically for a certain type of garment.

Flat pattern cutting and draping on the stand are two quite different techniques, but they can be combined to great advantage in the design room. A frequent problem for pattern cutters is to know how to construct a pattern for a part of a garment which is obviously easier to do on the dress stand. The technique of outlining the draped section on the dress stand, whether it be a whole bodice or simply a part of one, and checking it against the partly completed paper pattern, is covered on pp55-8. Ruched panels, bust shaping, cowl necklines and a draped party top are all demonstrated as part flat cut and part modelled designs.

The capsule wardrobe at the end of the book brings together the basic elements of a wardrobe for special occasions, mixing and matching classic garments in beautiful fabrics to cover a variety of occasions for day and evening.

One of the aims of this book is to dispel the belief that every design must be developed from the basic daywear block and to nurture the idea of having appropriate starter blocks to hand for specific styles. All the adjustments suggested for blocks can be applied to commercial patterns. In addition, by introducing small elements of draping into flat pattern cutting, I hope to stimulate interest in the art of modelling directly on the stand.

This book is intended for teachers and students at all levels from Foundation up to post graduate degree levels on design and manufacturing courses; up to A level in school; practising designers and pattern makers in the clothing industry, including those working in film and theatre, home dressmakers and designer dressmakers working from their own studios.

EQUIPMENT LIST

Pattern paper

Metre rule

Scissors: for cutting paper and card

Tape measure with both metric and imperial
measures

Short ruler

Set square: essential for obtaining right
angles on patterns and fabrics

Tracing wheel: for copying patterns and for
transferring lines from modelled fabric

French curve: useful for drawing smooth neck
and armhole lines and curved seams

Pencils: hard pencils are marked with an H
and produce fine, clear lines for pattern
making; soft pencils, marked HB, are best
for drawing and marking fabric

Dress stand

Calico for making toiles

Shears for cutting fabric

Narrow black stay tape [maximum width
7mm]: for taping design lines on the stand

Small scissors: for snipping into seam
allowances and trimming

Marking pen: a water soluble pen or soft
pencil is useful for marking toiles

Pins: long, fine pins are available for
modelling fine fabrics; lills, very short
pins, are useful for taping design lines on
the stand, sinking into the surface at an
angle and easily removed by pulling the
tape off the stand.

Pin cushion: strap to the wrist so you can use
both hands to hold fabric in position on
the stand during modelling

Weights: to hold down fabric, card or paper
patterns and prevent their moving when
being outlined

Stiletto or scriber: for puncturing small holes
in card

Notcher: clips out a small, narrow rectangle
[a notch] in fabric, blocks or patterns.

Notebook and file: for recording exercises

Needles and thread: for tacking up toiles

SET OF BASIC BLOCKS

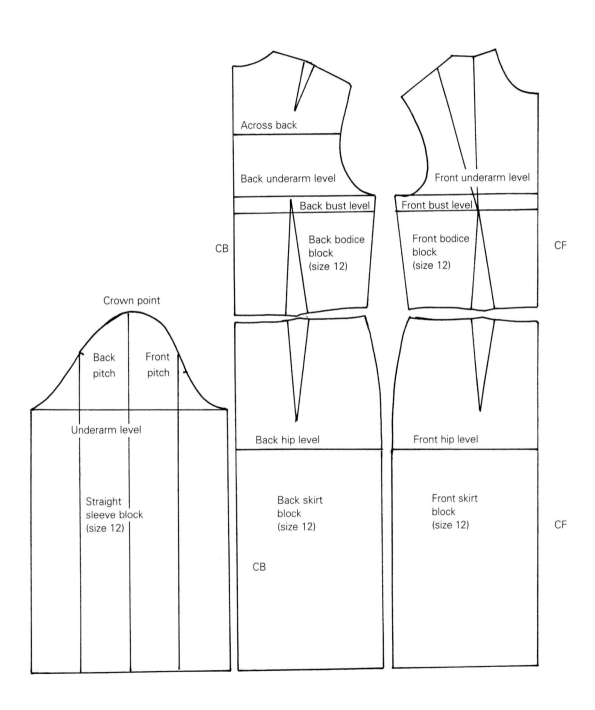

Across back

Back underarm level

Front underarm level

Back bust level

Front bust level

CB

Back bodice
block
(size 12)

Front bodice
block
(size 12)

CF

Crown point

Back
pitch

Front
pitch

Underarm level

Straight
sleeve block
(size 12)

Back hip level

Front hip level

Back skirt
block
(size 12)

Front skirt
block
(size 12)

CF

CB

TAKING MEASUREMENTS

The following measurements represent body size, not block size. The figures shown in the 'movement tolerance' column refer to the amounts already incorporated in the blocks to allow for normal body movement when wearing the garments. It is these amounts which will be changed when adapting the basic blocks to secondary blocks for developing close-fitting styles.

Size	8	10	12	14	16	18	Movement Tolerance	Size 12
Height	157.2 61	159.6 62½	162 63¾	164.4 64¾	166.8 65¾	169.2 66½		162 63¾
Neck	34 13⅜	35 13	36 14⅛	37 14	38 15	39 15⅜		36 14⅛
Across back	34 13⅜	35 13¾	36 14⅛	37 14½	38 15	39 15⅜	1.6 ⅝	37.6 14¾
Across chest	31.5 12½	32.5 12¾	33.5 13⅛	34.5 13½	35.5 14	36.5 14¼	0.6 ¼	34.1 13⅜
Underarm level	74 29	78 30	82 32¼	86 34	90 35½	94 37		82 32¼
Bust	80 31½	84 33	88 34¾	93 36½	98 38½	103 40½	10 4	98 38¾
Bust separation	16.8 6⅝	18 7⅛	19.2 7½	20.4 8	21.6 8½	22.8 9		19.2 7½
Under bust	61 24	66 26	71 28	76 30	81 32	86 34		71 28
Nape to back waist	38.8 15¼	40.4 15⅞	41 16⅛	41.6 16⅜	42.2 16⅝	42.8 16⅞		41 16⅛
Waist	60 23⅝	64 25¼	68 26⅝	73 28⅝	78 30⅝	83 32⅝	skirts 1 trousers 1 dresses 4 skirts ⅜ trousers ⅜ dresses 1¼	69 69 72 27 27 28⅛
High hip	80 31½	84 33	88 34¾	92 36¼	96 37¾	100 39⅜	4 1½	92 36¼
Hip	86 34	90 35½	94 37	98 38½	102 40⅛	106 41¾	5 2	99 39
Thigh	48.8 18⅞	51 20	54 21¼	57.4 22½	60.8 23⅝	63.2 24⅞		54 21¼
Knee	32.2 12⅝	33.6 13¼	35 13¾	36.4 14⅜	37.8 14⅞	39.2 15½	6 2½	41 16¼
Ankle	21.8 8⅝	22.4 8⅞	23 9	23.6 9⅜	24.2 9½	24.8 9¾	9 3½	32 12½
Shoulder	11.5 4½	11.7 4⅝	11.9 4⅞	12.1 4¾	12.3 4⅞	12.5 5		11.9 4⅞

Size	8	10	12	14	16	18	Movement Tolerance	Size 12
Outer sleeve	**56.2** 22	**57.1** 22½	**58** 22⅞	**58.9** 23⅛	**59.8** 23⅞	**60.7** 23⅞		**58** 22⅞
Armhole **38.6**	**40.6** 15⅛	**42.6** 16	**44.6** 16¾	**46.6** 17½	**48.6** 18⅜	19⅛		**42.6** 16¾
Bicep	**22.9** 9	**24.7** 9¾	**26.5** 10½	**28.3** 11⅛	**30.1** 11⅞	**31.9** 12½	**5** 2	**31.5** 12½
Elbow	**22.2** 8¾	**23.6** 9⅛	**25** 9⅞	**26.4** 10⅜	**27.8** 11½	**29.2** 11	**5** 2	**30** 11⅞
Wrist	**15** 6	**15.2** 6	**16** 6¼	**16.5** 6½	**17** 6⅝	**17.5** 6⅞	**6.5** 2½	**22.5** 8¾
Nape to ground	**140.4** 55½	**142.4** 56¼	**144** 57	**145.8** 57⅜	**147.6** 58½	**149.4** 59¼		**144** 57
Waist to hip	**19.4** 7⅝	**19.7** 7¾	**20** 7⅞	**20.3** 8	**20.6** 8⅛	**20.9** 8¼		**20** 7⅞
Waist to knee	**58.4** 23	**59.2** 23¼	**60** 23½	**60.8** 23⅞	**61.6** 24¼	**62.4** 24½		**60** 23½
Waist to floor	**100.4** 39½	**101.7** 40	**103** 40½	**104.3** 41	**105.6** 41½	**106.9** 42		**103** 40½
Body rise	**26.4** 10½	**27.2** 10⅞	**28** 11¼	**28.8** 11⅝	**29.6** 12	**30.4** 12⅜		**28** 11¼
Crotch depth	**61** 24¼	**63.5** 25¼	**66** 26¼	**68.5** 27¼	**71** 28¼	**73.5** 29¼	varies with style	**66** 26 ¾

1 Neck girth
2 Shoulder length
3 Across shoulders
4 Across back
5 Across chest
6 Underarm level
7 Over bust girth
8 Bust level girth
9 Under bust girth
10 Bust separation
11 Armhole girth
12 Waistline
13 High hip line
14 Hip widest part
15 Bicep
16 Elbow
17 Wrist
18 Thigh
19 Knee
20 Ankle
21 Full height
22 Nape to back waist
23 Nape to ground
24 Waist to hip
25 Waist to knee
26 Waist to floor
27 Body rise
28 Crotch length
29 Outer sleeve

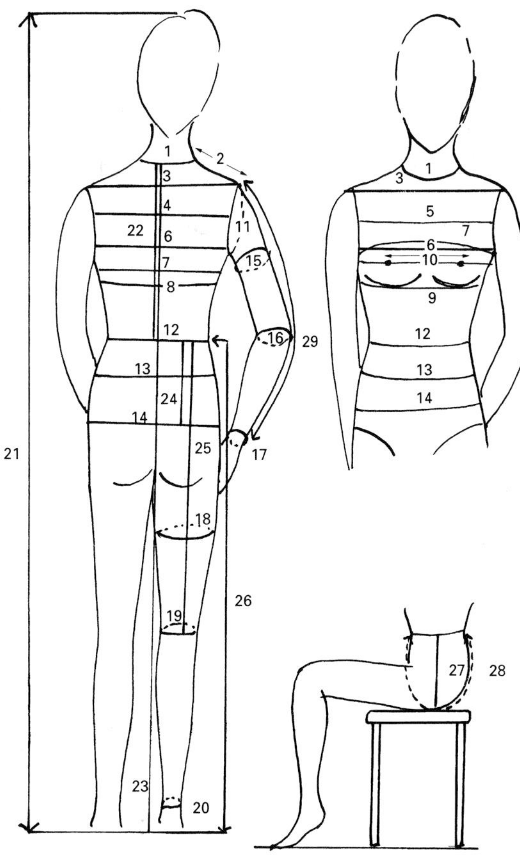

FABRICS

For all clothing, fabric is the essential ingredient. Deciding which fabric to use for special occasion clothes will mean considering the type of garment, when and where it will be worn, its structure – the design lines and fit – and the quality and characteristics of the desired fabric.

The dresses, long skirts, strapless bodices and bustiers in this book are mainly designed to be made in luxury fabrics. The jackets can be worn with skirts, trousers or dresses for both day and evening, the choice and quality of the fabric appropriate to the occasion.

When choosing fabrics, consider the pattern and texture as well as the fibre and weave. Printed fabrics obscure seamlines and darts, so are more appropriate in full-skirted dresses. Lace is more effective when not broken by seams and darts. Large patterns are lost in small garment areas and motifs interesting on the fabric roll are less so when broken by panel seams. Bustiers where the boned seams are the major focus are most effective when made in plain coloured but textured fabric.

Silk has always been considered the ultimate choice for special occasions. This 'Queen of fabrics' has many forms, from delicate, floaty chiffon and georgette to stiff and bouffant silks for full skirts and suit weight for skirts, jackets and coats. Many luxury fabrics now include elastomeric yarns which give varying degrees of stretch in woven as well as knitted fabrics. This allows us to reconsider previous design concepts: for instance, stretch lace removes the need for darts to shape the figure. The introduction of beads, sequins and other decoration into the weaving and knitting processes provides overall surface decoration which does not distract the eye in the way of many patterned fabrics.

Whatever the choice of fabric, due consideration must be given to the garment structure and the demands made on it in wear. 'Special occasions' may suggest fragile fabric but vigorous activities such as dancing require strongly made garments with seams that will withstand quite forceful body movements. Strapless bodices, however feminine, usually consist of several layers. A fragile outer layer should be underlined with a firm, but lightweight, closely-woven fabric strong enough to take the strain and to hold the boning in place.

The variety of luxury fabrics available provides designers with countless opportunities to combine more than one fabric in the visible, outer layer of many garment designs. Widely contrasting fabrics are teamed in the dresses shown on this page.

Far left The close-fitting dress with halter neck and bouffant frills uses taffeta for its crispness and ability to hold its shape, whether close to the body or gathered into frills. The gathered halter would be too stiff and bulky in the same fabric and a delicate chiffon adds a soft touch to the neckline. The otherwise simple style is enhanced by silk roses which disguise the horizontal seam in the skirt and emphasize the width of the frills.

Centre The satin of the skirt is teamed with a beaded stretch lace bodice, providing a stunning contrast. The dark top absorbs the light, whereas the satin fabric of the skirt catches it, giving off a lustrous sheen.

Far right A fitted plain silk bodice is enhanced by embroidery; beads at neckline and armhole catch the light and are scattered on the sides of the bodice. Ankle length, floating tulle echoes the beaded theme of the bodice in larger motifs scattered randomly through the skirt.

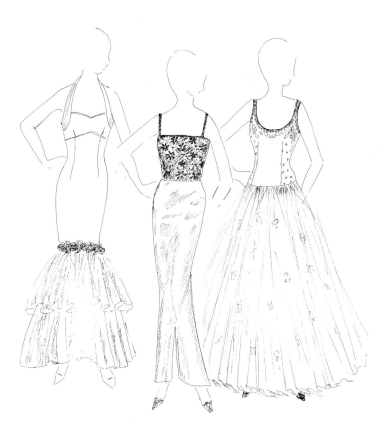

TRIMMINGS

Within the clothing industry, the term trimmings covers a wide range of haberdashery. In the context of this book, however, it implies added decoration or adornment which further enhances an already beautiful garment. This may include 'applied decoration', which is stitched on to the fabric of the garment, such as ribbons and braids, lace edgings and motifs, bows, roses and embroidery. It also includes piped seams and finely-bound edges which add a special touch but are constructed as an intrinsic part of the garment. The type of fastening used is also an important aspect of finishing a special garment and involves the search for exactly the right buttons or the covering of buttons with fabric to match a garment precisely.

There is now a wide range of beautiful trimmings to choose from in large stores and from manufacturers' catalogues. These include beads and diamanté fixed to narrow tape or ribbon which can be used to outline a seam or take the place of a shoulder band of fabric. Strips of gold or silver lace can become a bodice panel or are inserted the full length of a long sleeve. Metallic piped insertion tapes are very effective when emphasizing the seams of a strapless bodice.

When suitable trimmings cannot be found, a little imagination can work wonders. Cut around the outside edges of motifs from remnants of expensive embroidered fabrics and use them to decorate a top or skirt. Alternatively, use the narrow top border from an embroidered border fabric to edge the neckline and armholes of a sleeveless evening dress.

The garment and its trimming should work as one. The trimming is there only to complement the original choice of garment design and fabric.

Gold and silver cords, beds and embroidery can be very effective added to small areas of garments, as in the illustrations below.

1 Beads emphasize the flower motifs of the lace sleeve while beaded braid is shaped to follow the sleeve hemline.

2 Scalloped bodice hem outlined wth gold cord; and a row of beads add a luxurious touch.

3 Dangling beads draw attention to a simple bow, enhanced by a single silk rose. Many ribbons have a gold or silver selvedge, or tiny beads can be added to the edges of plain ribbon.

4 Clusters of pearls stitched to lace flower centres give an even richer contrast to the mainly chiffon draped bodice.

5 Close-up of the lace used for the bodice.

6 A purchased motif is used to decorate the shoulder of an asymmetrically styled dress. The upper and lower bodice edges are corded and emphasized by tiny beads to match those on the shoulder.

BLOCKS, SLOPERS, PATTERNS, SHELLS AND TOILES

'Block' is a pattern cutting term used in Great Britain and 'sloper' is its American equivalent. Both refer to two-dimensional templates, usually made from paper, card or plastic, which are used to develop patterns for garments in standard or individual measurements. Most blocks for womenswear include darts and shaped seams, which, when the block is copied in fabric and sewn together, take on the three-dimensional shape and fit of the human body of a particular size.

A 'pattern' is usually regarded as the completed set of shapes which represents a whole garment. Each piece should be marked with design number, size, name of section, how many pieces to cut and whether or not seam allowances have been included.

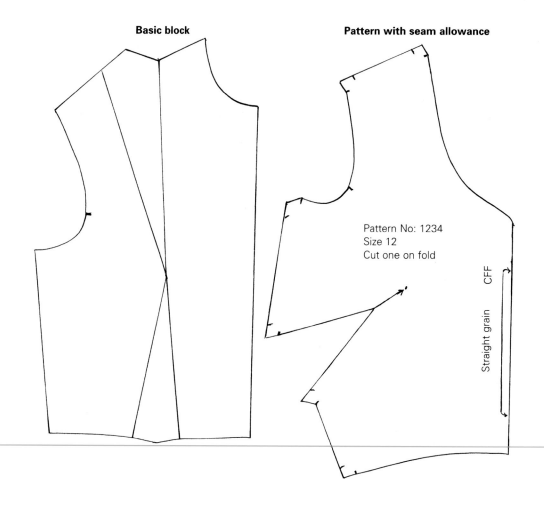

Basic block

Pattern with seam allowance

Pattern No: 1234
Size 12
Cut one on fold

Straight grain   CFF

The term 'shell' refers to a very simple shape, like a block, from which it differs by containing adjustable seam allowances so that it can be made up and tried on the person or dress stand. Shells are available from most commercial pattern catalogues and provide an alternative for those who have not come across 'blocks' (usually used in college or when working in the clothing industry).

A 'toile' is a copy of the pattern, or its main pieces, tacked up in an inexpensive fabric which as closely as possible duplicates the weight and characteristics of the final fabric intended for the garment.

The toile may have been cut from a pattern or draped directly on the stand. In either case its purpose is evaluation of the fit, proportion, hang and style details of the garment.

Shell

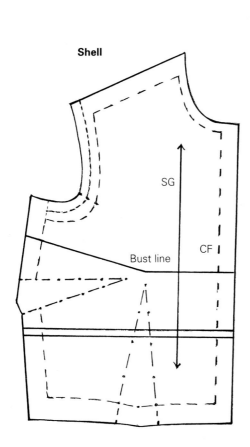

SG

CF

Bust line

Fitting a toile

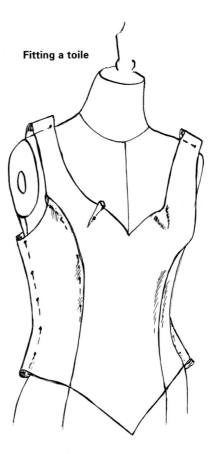

BASIC BLOCKS

A set of blocks for normal daywear is usually made up of five pieces: front and back bodice, front and back skirt and a sleeve. These blocks are known as primary, first or, more commonly, basic blocks. Fifth-scale representations of these can be found on p7 and they are used for the development exercises in this book. Other blocks can be developed from them; these are known as secondary blocks.

For the front and back bodice and the front and back skirt, only half of the body is represented, the right-hand side from centre back (or front) to the side seam position. All design lines for symmetric styling take place on this half. The final pattern also represents the right-hand side of the garment only and the pattern pieces are placed on double fabric to obtain a 'mirror image'. The exception to this is when an asymmetric design is being interpreted (see p54 for an asymmetric style draped on the dress stand and p70, where the whole of the front block is used to construct the wrapover skirt).

The sleeve block represents the whole arm because the front and back of the sleevehead are different in shape, the front being more rounded to accommodate the front arm muscle. Fitted sleeves also have darts, or ease, to accommodate the bent elbow, making the back seamline longer than the front.

When basic blocks are first obtained, only essential information is recorded on them, such as:

Type and name of block	Women's back skirt
Size	Size 12
Essential darts	These indicate the exact amount of suppression required to shape the two-dimensional flat shape to fit the three-dimensional human figure
Essential notches	Front and back pitch. Pitches are the balance marks on armhole and sleevehead for correctly inserting set-in sleeves.

There are no seam allowances on the blocks.

It can be helpful to add other marks, such as horizontal lines for the bust, underarm, across back, across front and hip level. It is also helpful to record the actual body measurements (not the same as 'size') and the amount of tolerance, which saves contstant rechecking during pattern construction stages. Sometimes the centre back and centre front of the bodice blocks are indicated. There are no grain lines on the blocks and except for the pitch marks, there should be no other notches. This makes sense becase every garment design is different and requires correctly placed grain lines and notches to suit the particular design. This is why grain lines and notches cannot be determined until the first stages of developing the block into a pattern. Seam allowances are only added in the very last stages of tracing off a final pattern (see p18).

Sleeveless bodices, contour-hugging styles and magyar, kimono and raglan styles are developed from the bodice blocks.
A trouser block may be constructed separately or developed from the skirt block.

Jacket and coat blocks may also be derived by adapting the primary blocks into what are known as 'soft tailored' suits and coats. This should not be confused with the special technique of drafting patterns to direct measurements used by tailors.

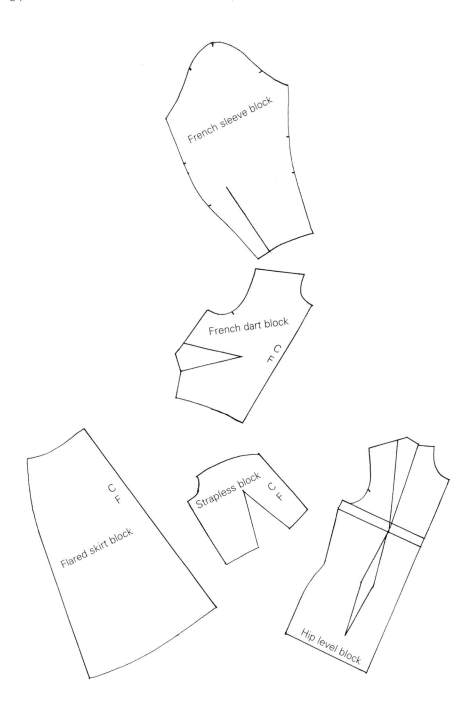

HOW TO USE THE BLOCKS IN THIS BOOK

No seam allowances have been added to these blocks. The outside lines represent the fitting or sewing line. Many changes are made to the copy of the block during its transition to a final pattern and a seam allowance gets in the way, causing confusion and inaccuracy. Seam allowances are added to the completed pattern pieces (the 'final pattern') and only if required. As they vary in width according to the choice of seam, fabric type and fabric thickness, many pattern cutters prefer to add the required amounts by marking them on to the fabric when cutting out.

All the exercises in this book can be developed from any basic blocks or commercial shells. It is not necessary to make all the secondary blocks. Use those which answer your needs at present. Classic style lines make a fresh appearance from time to time and blocks for those particular shapes can be made as required. If using a shell from a commercial pattern company, fold under (or remove) the seam allowances. Copy the pattern on to card and add the notches to make your own block.

In the clothing industry, where specialist machinery is available for seam neatening, 1cm (⅜") is allowed on most seams, 1.5cm-2cm (⅝"-¾") for open seams and 0.5cm (¼") on curved seams such as necklines and pocket edges. Commercial paper patterns allow 1.5cm (⅝") on all edges which is too wide for small curved edges and too narrow for open seams, particularly where a zip fastener is to be inserted. Facings require no seam allowance on the outer edges; they are simply neatened, usually by overlocking ('zig-zag' stitch). Bound edges need no seam allowance; it is the fitting line which is covered by the binding and seam allowance would make the garment larger.

It is well known that when a new style emerges it takes commercial pattern companies several months before the change can be seen in their catalogues. Many styles re-emerge, albeit in changed form, after a decade or more. It is a great advantage for pattern cutters and dressmakers to know how to develop such styles, whether from a block or a shell.

Once a garment design has taken shape in the designer's mind, usually after handling a fabric and draping it on the dress stand, a design sketch is drawn. The following list tracks the stages between the design sketch and the final pattern.

DESIGN SKETCH

Also known as a fashion sketch. The design is usually shown on an elongated figure. The sketch is not particularly detailed; it gives an impression with a suggestion of the main design lines.

WORKING SKETCH

A precisely detailed working drawing, with clear seamlines, neck shape, garment length, pocket positions. The working drawing often includes exact measurements for each part of the garment. It must be sufficiently detailed for a pattern cutter to produce a pattern which exactly interprets the original design. Not all designers are pattern cutters and the task of creating the pattern is often passed on to specialists.

MASTER PATTERN

This includes block development and construction stages, through to final adjustments to the design. It begins with using a set of blocks to outline a bodice, skirt and sleeve in the required size. There are no design lines at this stage, only darts which show how much shaping will be needed to fit a figure of that size.

Block development involves drawing on design lines, usually involving a change of dart position, the creation of extra seams, changing the neck shape and other details, including adding grain lines and notches but not facings or seam allowances. Several different stages of construction may take place according to the complexity of the garment, including tracing off sections, cutting them apart, folding out darts and creating flares pleats or gathers. The altered pieces are replaced on the master plan and the new shape redrawn.

When all the construction stages have been completed, the master pattern appears to be very complicated, with many lines overlapping. Using different colour pens will make it easier to trace off the individual pattern pieces. The main pattern pieces, still without seam allowances, are then cut out in an inexpensive fabric, such as calico. Seam allowances are marked directly onto the fabric, with extra allowed for adjustments. Facings, interlinings and seam neatening are not necessary at this 'toile' stage - the fitting of the garment on the dress stand or a live model. The garment is machine tacked, fitted, evaluated and any adjustments made. It is then un-picked, alterations transferred to the master pattern and facings added where needed.

FINAL PATTERN

The corrected pattern pieces are traced off for the last time, hems and seam allowances added, notches, grainlines, foldlines, centre front and centre back and other details recorded. Other essential information includes the design number, size, name of pattern piece, how many to cut. The pattern pieces are counted and given numbers, then each pattern piece marked appropriately eg 1 of 2 pieces.

BASIC BLOCKS AS GARMENT TEMPLATES

Blocks can be likened to the templates used for making elaborate patchwork quilts. These are available in many shapes: square, diamond, hexagon. It saves the quiltmaker a great deal of time and effort to be able to choose a template of the appropriate shape for each section rather than continually to re-shape the original square or rectangle.

It is the same with garment blocks. The original, the basic block, is the starting template. Once its possibilities and its limitations are understood, it becomes easy to judge when it can be used in its original shape and when a different shape block should be chosen.

Basic blocks for womenswear are used for variations of skirts, blouses and dresses for day and special occasionwear.

BODY TOLERANCE IN THE BASIC BLOCKS

Blocks are constructed to body measurements plus sufficient tolerance (extra room) to allow for normal body movement and for the garment to be worn over underwear. To work out how much tolerance has been added to the block or other basic pattern you are using, fill in a chart like the one below. Measure the block across the whole width from centre back to centre front (½ the bust width), double it to get the full bust width, then subtract the body measure. The difference equals the amount of tolerance at bust level.

	Body measurement	Block measurement	Amount of tolerance included
Bust			
Waist			
Hip			

Most blocks allow 10cm (4⅝") more than body measurement at bust and hip levels and 4cm (1⅝") at the waist of a dress (only 1cm [⅜"] on a separate skirt or trousers). This may sound generous, but when sewn in fabric is quite a close fit.

The tolerance allowed at bust and waist levels affects other areas of the bodice: ample room in the front armhole area suits the set-in type of sleeve but is too loose for sleeveless styles and the comfortable fit of a bodice with a fairly high neckline becomes too loose if the neckline is cut low.

Sleeve blocks come in three shapes: straight, semi-fitted and fitted. All have to be wide enough to allow the arm to bend. The sleevehead must be shaped to fit the armhole of the bodice with sufficient 'ease' to be sewn into the garment and look attractive. There must be enough room under the arm to allow it to be raised without tearing or pulling up the side seam of the garment.

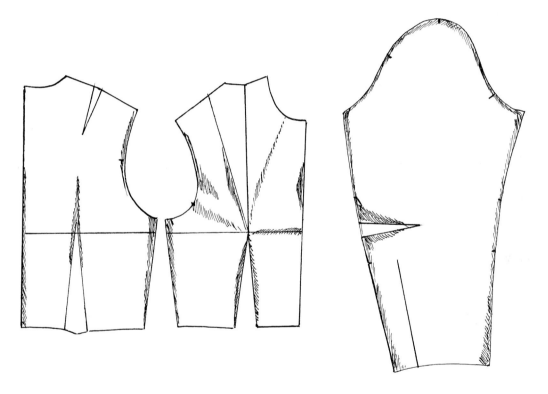

Shaded areas show where tolerance is allowed

The bodice underarm seam is rarely seen in size charts because it is difficult to determine exactly where the armhole level begins. The body armhole is higher than the garment armhole and the underarm points of the bodice and sleeve are positioned low to provide ample room for full arm movement inside the garment.

CHANGING DART POSITIONS

The basic blocks in this book use darts to shape fabric to the body contours. Working with blocks involves the changing of darts from one place to another, sometimes as part of the design or else temporarily, to clear a space for drawing the design lines, after which the dart may be returned to the original position or be 'folded out' and allowed to disappear into a design seam.

Darts can be relocated in any position. Study the diagram of possible locations and try some of the following exercises. Use either the 'slash and spread' or the pivoting method. Both will be found necessary in complicated styles (see pp24 and 35).

One thing remains constant: the dart is needed to create the three-dimensional garment shape and retain the size of the original block.

All darts start at an outside edge and end at the bust point otherwise the pattern cannot remain absolutely flat which is necessary for cutting out fabric laid on the table.

Whether the dart is pivoted or the slash and spread method is used, the whole of the dart to the bust point must be incorporated.

Some blocks include a mark for the dart end 1.5cm (⅝") from the bust point. This is to show where the dart is shortened on the final pattern piece for the machinist to stop sewing. Pattern cutters must disregard this sewing mark during these initial stages until finalizing the pattern with sewing instructions. To avoid confusion, this dart is omitted from the blocks in this book.

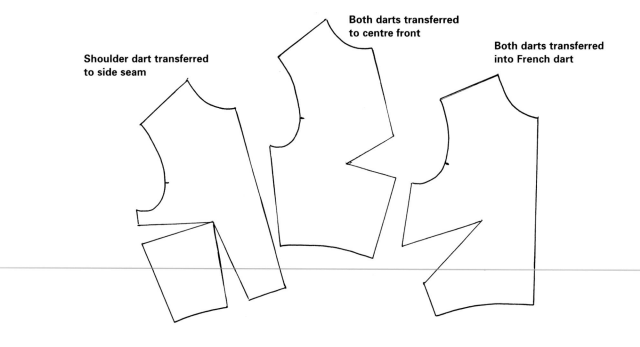

Shoulder dart transferred to side seam

Both darts transferred to centre front

Both darts transferred into French dart

Dart positions on front bodice block

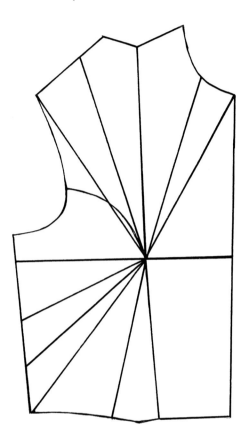

**Final pattern shows
shortened dart for sewing**

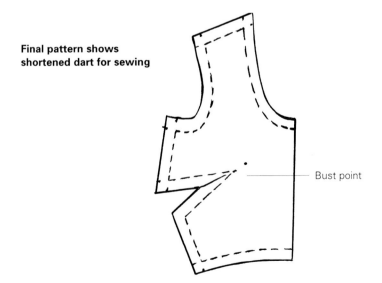

Bust point

Slash and spread method

This is a time and energy consuming method but it is essential to be aware of it because there are occasions when the quicker method of pivoting the dart is not possible, such as when the design lines do not go through the pivot (bust) point. See p27 for solutions to pivoting curved darts and for creating curved seams.

1 Trace the block, including the darts, onto a fresh piece of paper. Remove block.
2 Draw a line representing the new dart position and cut the line to the bust point.
3 Close the dart to be changed. A new dart appears as a space.
4 Redraw the block and draw in new dart, or glue a piece of paper under the space.

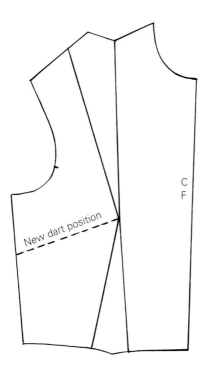
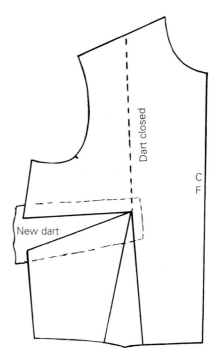

Pivoting method

Pivoting is a method of controlling the bust point on paper by outlining the block and swivelling it to close out darts and reposition them elsewhere. This is a very quick and accurate method of transferring darts from one position to another. It is necessary to make a hole in all dart points so the pencil point can penetrate. Depending on the position of the new dart, the block is tilted either clockwise or anti-clockwise. The exercises in the right-hand-side column on p26 show anti-clockwise pivoting.

For a special technique when pivoting curved darts see p27.

On the front bodice block make a hole in the bust point. Try changing the shoulder dart into the side seam. It may be helpful to insert a paper pin in the bust point to secure it to the paper.

1 Mark the new dart end on the side of the block.
2 Outline the block edge; this will not change. Start at the neck edge of the shoulder dart, continue clockwise, marking the ends of the waist dart until you reach and mark the new dart position.
3 Swivel the block clockwise to close out the shoulder dart. Mark along the shoulder (anti-clockwise) round the armhole to the new dart. Remove the block and draw dart legs.

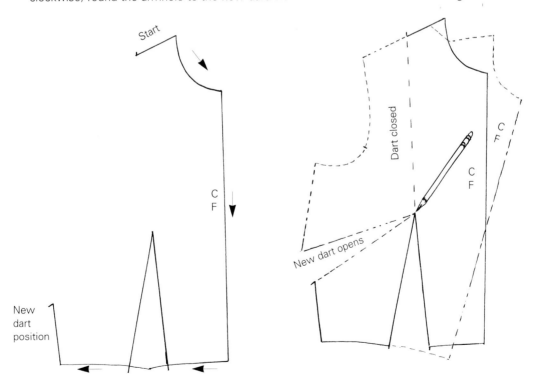

Once you are familiar with the pivoting method, try some of the following exercises. Some involve moving only one dart, in others both darts change position. Remember to start by drawing round the part unaffected by the change.

Pivoting exercises

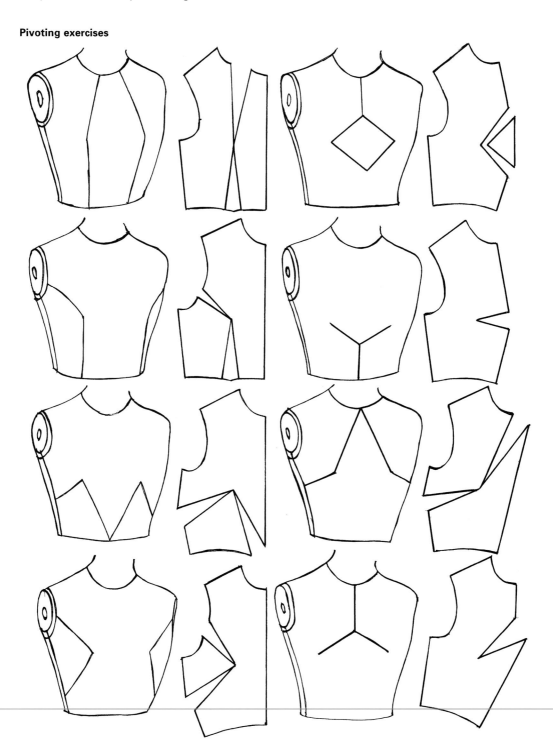

Pivoting curved darts

1 Draw a curved dart on the block.
2 Use an awl to make small holes along the curve.
3 Pivot the block as for straight darts but in addition to marking the block outer edge, pencil in the extra holes. Pivot and close first one dart, then the second.
4 Remove the block. Join the pencil dots into a curve.

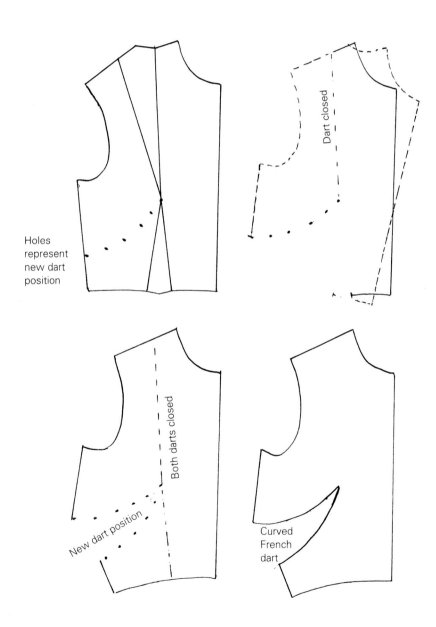

Holes represent new dart position

Dart closed

Both darts closed

New dart position

Curved French dart

SECONDARY BODICE BLOCKS

The main purpose of this book is to show pattern cutters how to make secondary blocks and to use them to develop particular types of garment designs. Having a block already adjusted to a tight fit throughout the bodice, including neckline and armhole, saves the designer of close-fitting party and eveningwear from making these alterations to a basic block every time a pattern is required for a new style. If you start from the basic blocks for every new design, it is easy to forget to make adjustments or the exact amounts to be changed and it is not possible to do so once the garment has been cut. Secondary blocks save time and energy by already being the correct fit.

Sleeveless styles and bodices with low or wide necklines occur frequently in designs for special occasion clothes. However, not all sleeveless styles have low necklines and many bodices with low necklines have sleeves. It is sensible, therefore, for the busy designer dressmaker to have several blocks and to choose the most appropriate one for the design in mind.

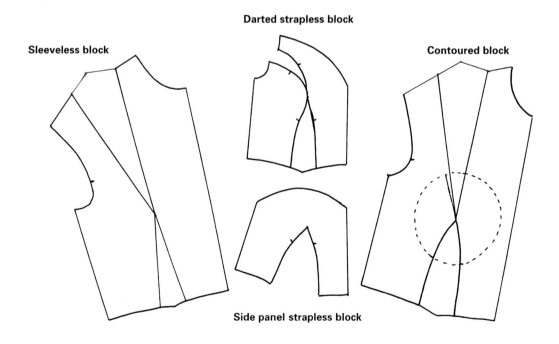

Darted strapless block

Sleeveless block

Contoured block

Side panel strapless block

Garment type	Name of Secondary Block	What changes	Result
Bodices with sleeveless armhole	Tightened armhole block	1cm (⅜") dart inserted from lower armhole to bust point. Side seams raised 1cm (⅜") and reduced 1cm (⅜").	The remainder of the bodice retains normal fit for daywear. Suitable for party and evening dresses; summerwear.
Low/wide necklines	Tightened neckline block	1cm (⅜") dart inserted from front neckline to bust point, removing surplus fabric in chest area.	The remainder of the bodice retains normal fit for daywear, including the armholes. Suitable for party, evening, bridalwear.
Sleeveless and low neckline	Tightened armhole and neckline block	Both the above alterations combined in one new block.	Can only be used for sleeveless styles with low necklines., never with set-in sleeves. Suitable for party and eveningwear.
Styles with very close fit at bustline and through midriff area, plus sleeveless and low neckline	Contoured block	Both the above alterations plus increasing the block darts, adding a centre front cleavage dart and defining the bust 'cup'; increasing back dart.	Very close fitting bodice block. Suitable for party and eveningwear and as a basis for bustiers and boned bodices, strapless styles. Suitable for very close-fitting party, evening and bridalwear.

TIGHTENED ARMHOLE BLOCK

> **Design note**
>
> A tightened block armhole is no longer suitable for styles with set-in sleeves.

1 Outline the back and front basic bodice blocks, including darts and armhole notches.
  Mark a new dart on front only, 1cm (⅜") wide starting 4cm (1½") from the underarm point
  along the armhole. Draw dart legs to bust point.

2 On both back and front blocks, move the underarm points in 1cm (⅜") and up 1cm (⅜").
  Connect in a smooth curve to armhole. Redraw side seams to normal side waist points.

3 Pivot the underarm dart into the shoulder or waist dart. The armhole is smaller. The amount of
  block suppression has not changed, only its position.

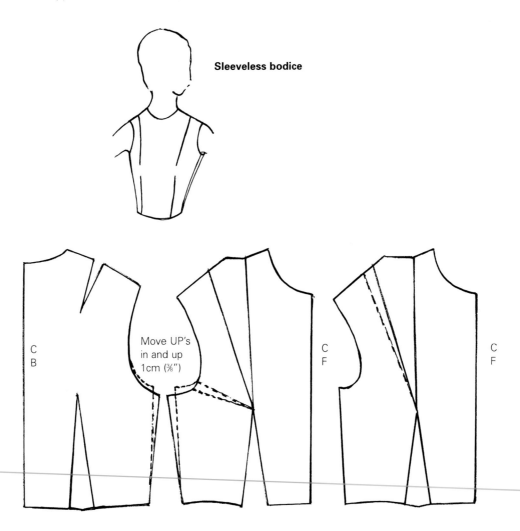

Sleeveless bodice

Move UP's
in and up
1cm (⅜")

C
B

C
F

C
F

TIGHTENED NECKLINE BLOCK

> **Design note**
>
> A tightened neckline must always be cut low. It is now too narrow and too tight to fit a normal neck or the neckline of the dress stand.

Only the front bodice block neckline is tightened for this block. The armholes are unchanged and remain suitable for any set-in sleeve.

1 Outline the front basic block only, including darts and armhole notches. Mark a new dart 1cm (⅜") wide, starting 4cm (1½") from base of front neck. Draw dart legs to bust point.

2 Pivot the neck dart into the shoulder or waist dart. The neckline is smaller. The amount of block suppression has not changed, only its position.

Tightened neckline block

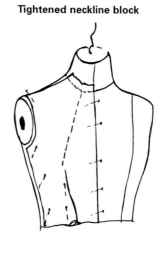

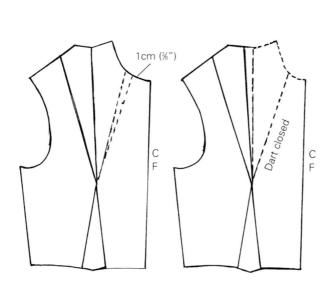

COMBINED TIGHTENED ARMHOLE AND NECKLINE BLOCK

> **Design note**
>
> It makes no difference which basic block you use. The original darts may be one or more, usually a waist dart and a shoulder dart, or a single waist dart. The amount of tolerance removed is exactly the same.

The previous two secondary blocks each dealt with one aspect of tightening, either the armhole or the neckline, thus avoiding a loose front armhole or a gaping front neckline.

This combined block is the ideal starting point for garments which feature low necklines with sleeveless armholes, such as party and evening dresses and sun dresses. The combined block includes both the extra darts which are pivoted into the block's existing darts, leaving the block ready for developing the pattern.

1   Draw both new darts onto a basic block. Reduce the side seams by 1cm (⅜") and raise them by 1cm (⅜"). Redraw the armhole.
2   Both new darts pivoted into two existing bodice darts.
3   Both new darts pivoted into a single waist dart.

Combined tightened armhole and neckline block

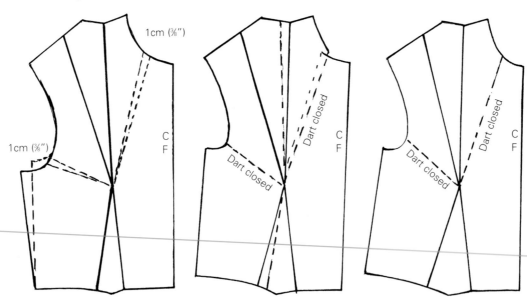

CONTOURED BLOCK

This very close-fitting block adds a tightened midriff and a centre front 'cleavage' dart. It produces bodices which are a very close fit round the bust area and rib cage. It is also the basis of the strapless bodice block described on page 38. The extra shaping can be drawn onto the combined tightened armhole and neckline block and used or ignored according to the design.

The contoured block is used only for sleeveless, low-neck styles with a tight midriff. The tightened waist dart follows the bust contour. The lower half of the bust circle is a guide for the bra sections of lingerie, swimwear and bustiers and indicates the position for underwiring.

1   Draw a horizontal line at front bust level.
2   Raise the height of the back dart to across back level.
3   Draw in centre front 'cleavage' dart 0.5cm (¼") each side of the bust level line.
4   Draw a circle 8cm (3") in diameter around the bust point.
5   Increase waist dart 0.5cm (¼") on both sides from bust point to nothing at normal position and on one side only from bust point to top of bust circle.

Contoured block

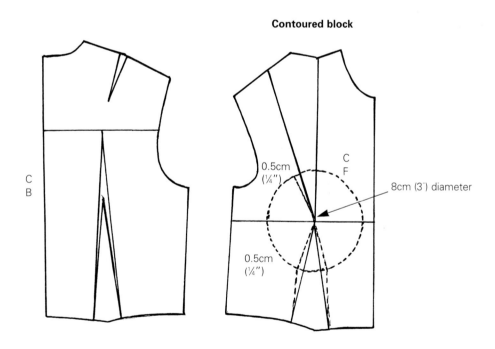

Use the back and front contoured bodice blocks for the examples on this page and on the page opposite. These blocks already have the armhole, neckline and midriff tightened, so no further adjustment is necessary before drawing on the design lines (only the front is shown).

In the first example, the shoulder dart has been pivoted into the armhole by the curved dart method described on page 27. Draw on the neckline and add notches and grainlines.

In the second example, the curved dart is taken below the bust and ends in a short, straight dart to the bust point. Pencil the line you wish the new dart to take onto the contoured block as a single line (the dart will be created by the pivoting). Puncture the marked line, then pivot the shoulder and waist darts into the new dart shape, which will appear where the pencil penetrates the holes.

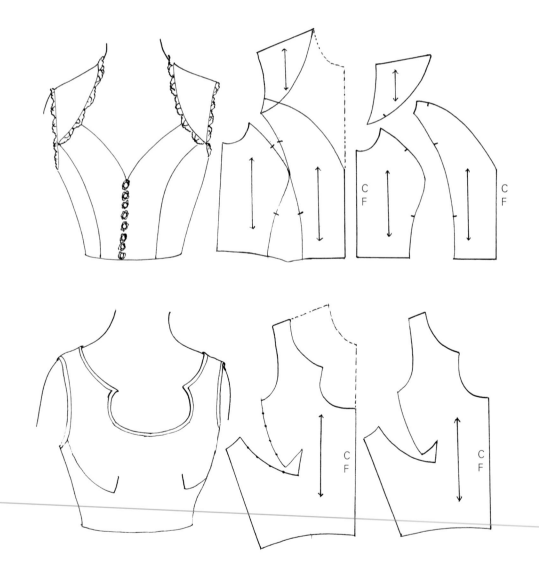

Design note

For designs with normal high necklines and set-in sleeves, use the basic block. Draw on the tightened waist darts up to the bust point.

The example with the diamond shape in the bodice has both bodice darts re-directed into the centre front. The lower bodice front will be placed on a fold of fabric. The diamond comes apart from the bodice and is cut separately, also on a fold. All the dart control is now in the diamond shape and the bodice will fit very closely to the midriff.

In the lower example, both bodice darts have been re-directed to the waist, creating a very large dart, which is folded out of the midriff section but remains as small gathers in the seam under the bust.

The darts in the contoured blocks contain the original darts from the basic blocks, the extra darts created to tighten the armhole and neckline, plus the extra tightening of the bust circle. It is noticeable in the four designs shown that the darts are much larger and more shaped than the darts of the basic blocks. More fabric has been 'taken in', creating a very close fit.

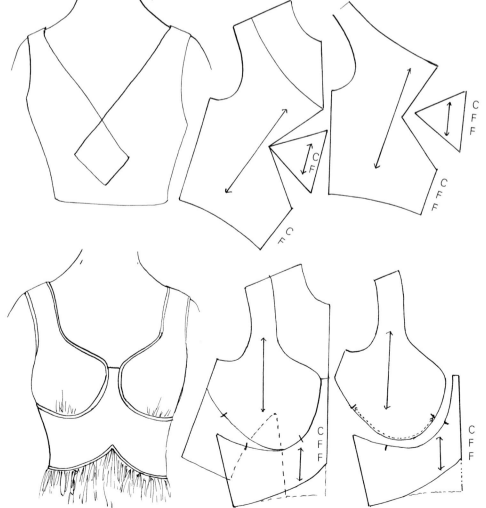

STRAPLESS BODICE BLOCKS

There are two main types of strapless block: one with no armhole shaping and one with half an armhole. The fit of the armhole is snug in the first type and varies in the second, depending on whether or not sleeves are introduced (see chart below). Darts, panel lines and other design features may be used to give variety.

Bodice type	Bodice fit	Armhole fit	Sleeves
No armhole	Very snug	Close to body	No set-in sleeve but may wear separate sleeves
Half an armhole	As above but more tolerance at upper side seams	Not close to body but higher than armholes in daywear	May have half a sleeve or a full sleeve supported by elastic or wiring at the shoulder
Half an armhole	Very snug	No sleeves	Separate sleeves may be worn

* Separate sleeves are discussed on p60.

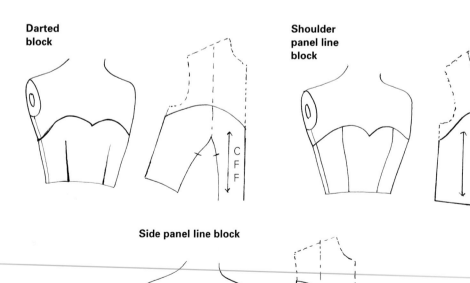

Darted block

Shoulder panel line block

Side panel line block

Strapless blocks are developed from the contoured bodice block. The neckline and armhole are already tightened, the bust cup and other details recorded, ready for use.

The diagrams below show where to introduce the design lines for the three main classic strapless bodices: darted, shoulder panel line and side panel line. The upper edges can easily be adjusted to different shapes. Add these three blocks to your block collection and use them as the starting point for any strapless styles.

All strapless bodices need support, usually boning, to keep them in place on the body. These are positioned on, or close to the main seams, on an inner layer of the bodice, except in bustiers, where they are shown on the outside as a design feature.

Half armhole strapless block with sleeves

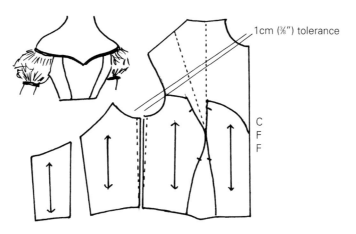

1cm (⅜") tolerance

C F F

Sleeveless strapless block

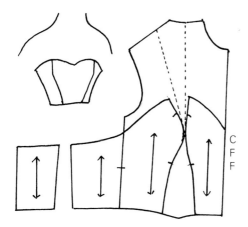

C F F

Half armhole strapless block without sleeves

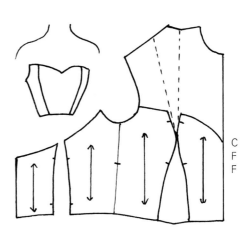

C F F

The following sketches and their 'masterplans' are based on the three previous classic designs with extra panels or shaping. Many effects are possible with the same design lines by the choice of different fabrics and trimmings. For designs which come below the waist, use the contoured hip block which can be traced from the dress block. (see p45).

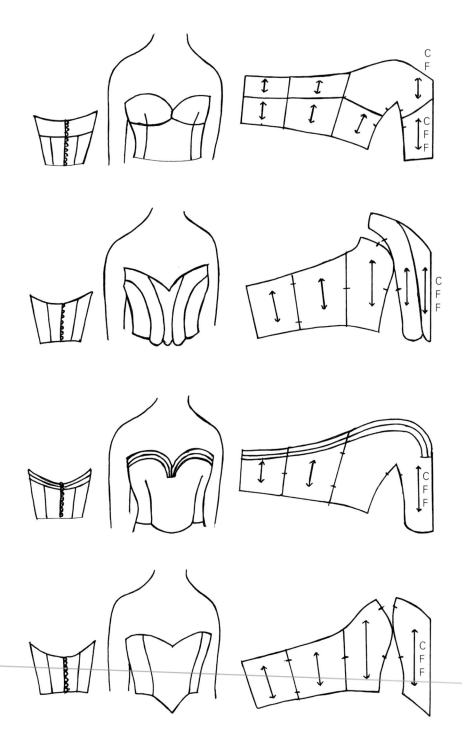

Strapless bodices may fasten at centre back, centre front or left side seam. Zips, buttons and lacings may be used. Add buttonstands for buttons and buttonholes but make the following adjustments for loop fastenings and lacings.

Button and loop fastening

To avoid the opening becoming off centre because the loops extend beyond the centre seam, cut a strip (the width of the loop) off the left hand side centre back bodice. Add the same amount to the right-hand side so that the buttons sit exactly on the centre.

Lacing

To ensure a snug fit, cut 2cm (¾") off each side of the centre back or centre front seamline. The laces pull the garment to close the gap.

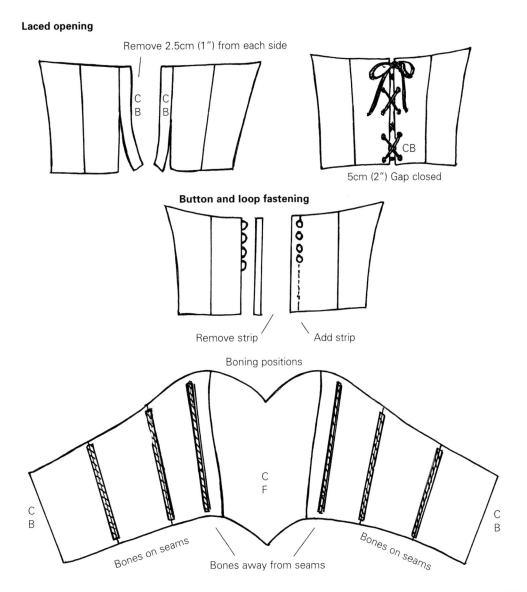

Laced opening

Remove 2.5cm (1") from each side

5cm (2") Gap closed

Button and loop fastening

Remove strip   Add strip

Boning positions

Bones on seams   Bones away from seams   Bones on seams

BUSTIERS

Some bustiers belong in the strapless category, others have shoulder seams and may be sleeveless or have set-in sleeves. Like other boned bodices, they may end above, on or below the waistline.

Rules apply for choice of starter block.

Type	Starter block	Additional adjustment
Bustiers with sleeves	Tightened neckline block [normal armhole]	Midfiff tightening plus tighten lower ⅔ seam
Sleeveless bustiers	Tightened neckline and armhole block	
Strapless [no armhole]	Strapless block	
Strapless with ½ armhole (with sewn in sleeve)	Strapless block	Must allow some ease on upper ⅔ side seam

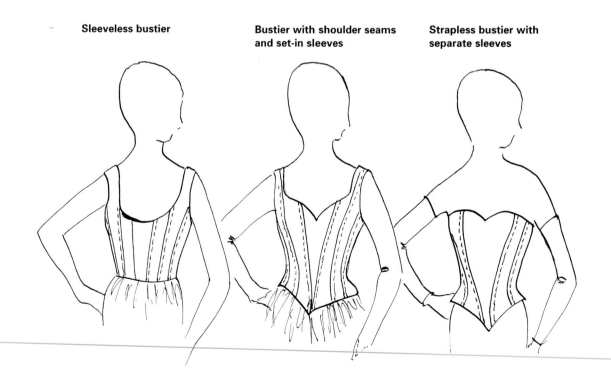

Sleeveless bustier   **Bustier with shoulder seams and set-in sleeves**   **Strapless bustier with separate sleeves**

In bodices with more than one panel line, the dart control can be divided between the seams. This reduces the drastic shaping needed for a tight fit in many bodices. In the bustier shown, the front waist dart is divided between the two panel lines.

Measure the front waist dart at the waistline and divide the figure by two. Put half of this amount each side of the panel lines. For example: a 6cm (2½") waist dart divided by two = 3cm (1¼"). Put 1.5cm (⅝") on each side of the two panel lines.

Classic bustier with boned seamlines, deep 'V' point at centre front and centre back

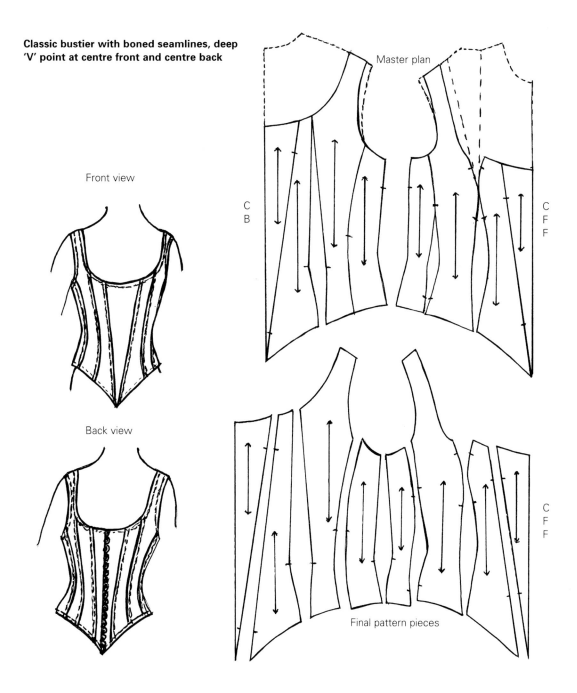

Front view

Back view

Master plan

Final pattern pieces

Top bustier Use contoured block. Transfer shoulder dart to armhole. Remove 2.5cm (1″) strip at centre front. Close remainder of back dart.

Centre bustier Extend strapless block below waist. Draw on design lines with lower flare. Trace off side cups and add to centre front cups.

Lower bustier Extend strapless block below waist. Draw curved lower edge and side panel lines. Add flare to side panel and side seams.

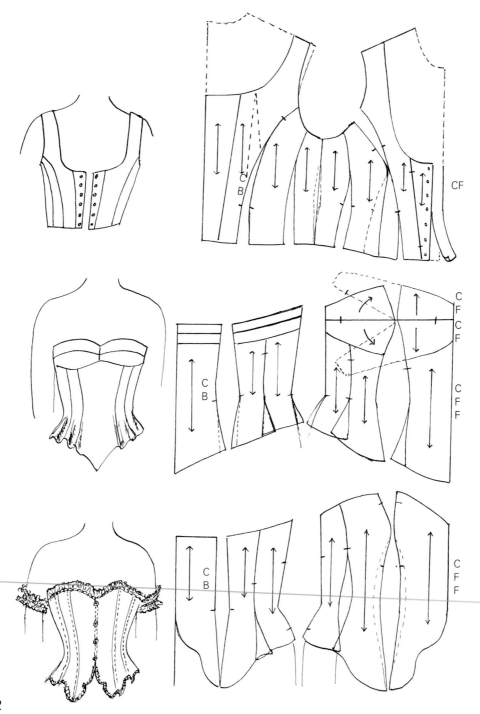

Bustier inspired by a Medieval bodice

1   Outline the block, transferring the shoulder and waist darts to the centre front at bust level. Lower the centre front line for the end of the panel.

2   Draw the neckline from the armhole to the centre front. Draw the design line from the side seam, in a curve under the bust towards the front and complete the centre front panel below the waistline. Draw a short slash line from the bust point to the design line. Mark a notch a few centimetres each side of this line.

3   Trace off the whole of the centre front panel, cut the short slash line to the bust point and close the centre front dart. The dart control will be transferred to the under bust area and becomes ease (or a dart if preferred). Paste a piece of paper under the gap. Replace the pattern piece on the master pattern, aligning the centre fronts, and add a straight grain line parallel to the centre front.

4   Draw the band on the centre back. The sides of the dart become a seam. Draw a band on the sleeve block. This will require elastic to keep it on the arm or it can be narrowed as required.

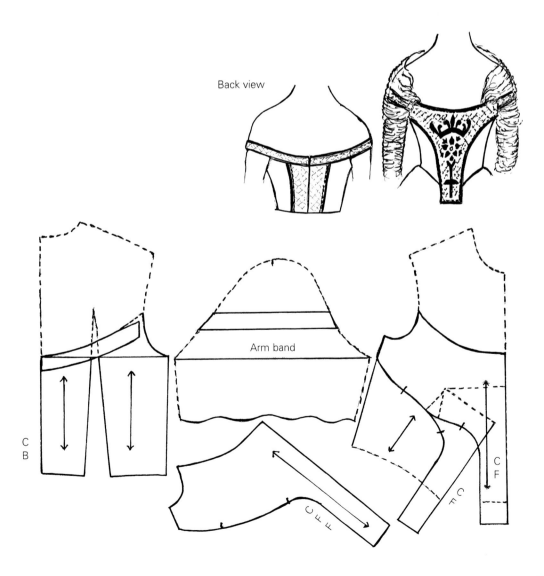

Back view

Arm band

C
B

C
F

SECONDARY DRESS BLOCKS

Instructions are given here for a dress block to knee level; this can be extended for longer dresses. The cut-off line 20cm (8") below the waistline is for a separate hip-length bodice block.

A dress block can be constructed by combining the bodice and skirt blocks. The bodice of the dress may be the basic block or any of the secondary blocks developed from it. If you use the basic bodice block, the resulting dress block will be appropriate for all normal daywear and eveningwear with a high neckline and set-in sleeves but will require adaptation for low necklines, sleeveless styles and contoured styling.

Designers and pattern cutters making patterns for party and evening dresses would benefit from using the secondary bodice blocks to construct their dress blocks. Clearly labelled, the appropriate dress block is immediately to hand, ready for the new design lines without the need for major preliminary adjustments.

The dress block, like the bodice block, can be constructed for a variety of purposes. It can be traced off to hip level which is very useful for blouses and for adaptation to a jacket block. It can also be lengthened to any point down to the ankle.

The dress block may also incorporate the same variety of bodice fittings as the bodice block itself. The exception to this is the waist fit which needs to be a little looser in the dress block to allow normal actions like bending and reaching.

The following blocks would be useful for the designer of evening and partywear dresses, making a variety of dress designs and saving valuable time in adapting the basic dress block which is only suitable for fairly high necklines and set-in sleeves.

Sleeveless dress block   (still suitable for high necklines)
Low neckline dress block (still takes a set-in sleeve)
Combined sleeveless and low neckline dress block
Contoured dress block   (all the above plus midriff shaping)
Strapless dress block with half an armhole (will take half and full sleevehead)
Strapless dress block without an armhole (not suitable for sleeves, except the 'separate' sleeve)
Side panel strapless dress block (1) designed to take sleeves
Side panel strapless dress block (2) worn without sleeves or with separate sleeves

BASIC DRESS BLOCK

1 Outline bodice and skirt blocks between two parallel lines as shown. Ignore the skirt waist darts.

2 Draw in hip, bust and underarm lines. The waistline shown is a guide only. This is a one-piece block from shoulder to hem and has no waist seam. The side waist points of bodice and skirt should meet. This creates a small gap between the bodice and skirt at centre back and centre front waist, which is inevitable if the straight grain is maintained.

3 Draw in the skirt waist darts immediately beneath the bodice darts.

Front view

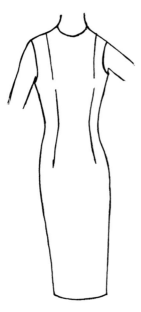

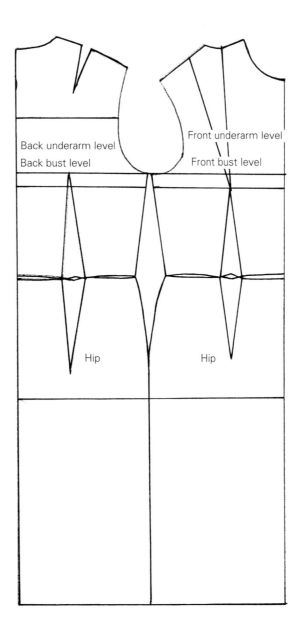

Back underarm level

Back bust level

Front underarm level

Front bust level

Hip

Hip

Back

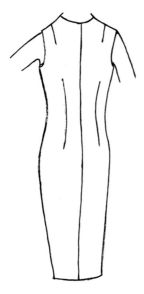

DESIGNS FROM THE ONE-PIECE DRESS BLOCK

The one-piece, darted dress block can be used for simple styles with straight or slightly-flared skirts. The shoulder dart is usually connected to the waist dart through the bust point, making one long dart, or is transferred into the armhole, becoming curved and joining the waist dart as in a 'side panel line'. It can also be directed into the side seam.

This block may be used for dresses cut on the straight grain or the bias. Bias fabric behaves quite differently from fabric cut on the straight grain. It clings to the body contours and falls softly. In long dresses the designer wishing to cut on the bias is limited by the fabric width. The 'true cross', that is, the bias cut at an angle of 45 degrees from the straight grain, cuts across the cloth diagonally, restricting the length to be cut.

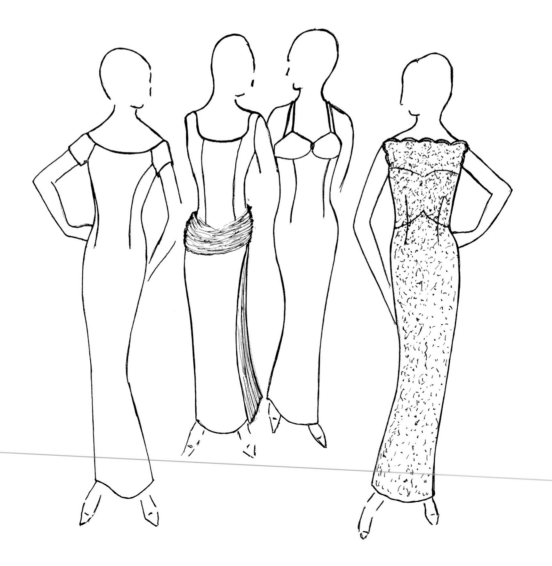

Depending on which secondary bodice block has been used to create the dress block, all the former variations of neckline, armhole and contour shaping can be achieved. For increasing the lower width for body movement (such as dancing), consider flare (pp 50-51) and godets and fishtails (pp 66-9).

The eight dresses on this spread are all developed from one-piece dress blocks using most of the variations of secondary bodice blocks suggested. The following blocks were used.

Page 46, left to right: Dress block with tightened neckline, tightened midriff and normal armhole; Combined sleeveless and tightened neckline block with tightened midriff; Strapless block (no armhole); Strapless block for the foundation dress, sleeveless block for over-dress

This page, left to right: Contoured block; Strapless block (no armhole) plus draped overlay on bust; Strapless block (no armhole), plus shoulder drape; Contoured block

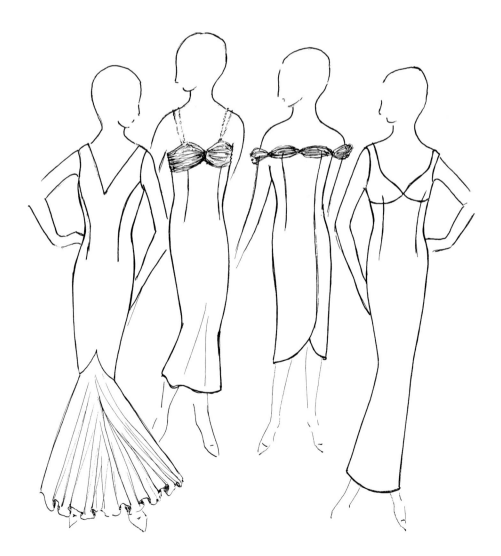

PRINCESS-LINE DRESS BLOCK

The princess seams run from mid-shoulder or armhole to the hemline, following the body contours. Cut shorter for hip block or short dress block. The seams allow the hem to be widened evenly throughout the garment. The required hem width is divided between the side and panel line seams and centre back and front seams if not placed on a fold. Consider the limitations imposed by the fabric width when calculating amounts to be added to each seam, especially in floor length garments.

The princess line block has no waist seam, but horizontal seams can be introduced above and below the waist. This can be seen in the Empire line (pp50-51), the dress on p89, the top on p91 and two of the jackets on p93.

The number of seams running through the waist curve enable the waist tolerance to be evenly spread throughout the garment, creating a smooth effect.

Flare lines are shown on the block as a suggestion for increasing hem width. However, the dress can also be straight if provision is made for 'walking' or 'stride' room. Splits and vents are less attractive than in the one-piece block. Consider grown-on godets or godets in the seams (see pp68-9).

1   Extend one-piece dress block to length required.
2   Connect the shoulder and waist darts from mid-shoulder and through the bust point.
3   Draw flare lines from the skirt dart points to the hem.
4   Calculate hem width required. If in its straight version, the total hem width is 96cm (38"), it will be 48cm (19") on the half pattern. To double this, mark a point 8cm (3⅛") from each side of the side seams and panel seams.
5   Connect these points to the waist darts at least 10cm (4") above the hip level to allow sufficient ease over hips. The waist can be further reduced through centre back and centre front when not placed on a fold.

Design note:

The vertical seams of the Princess line are flattering, giving an illusion of height. For eveningwear, the effect is even more dramatic in a floor length dress, whether widely flared or tapered and ending in a fishtail (see pp66-7).

Front

Back

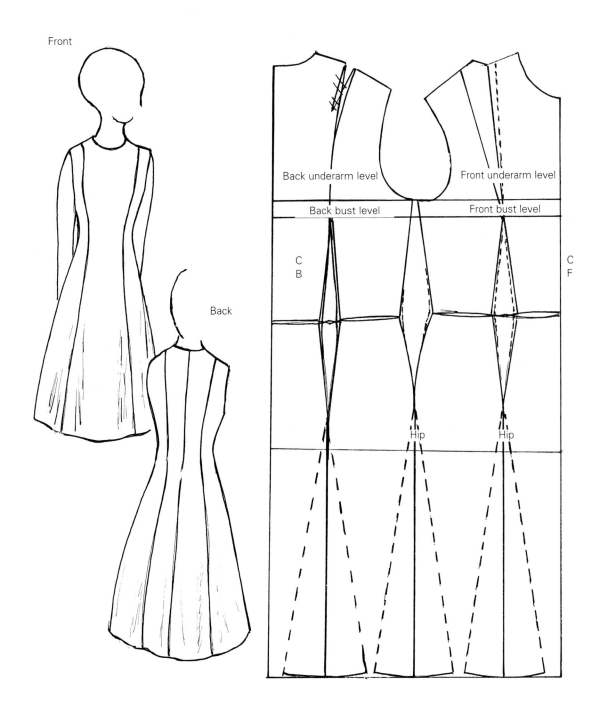

Back underarm level

Front underarm level

Back bust level

Front bust level

C
B

C
F

Hip

Hip

EMPIRE-LINE DRESSES

The Empire line features a horizontal seamline beneath the bust and may be used in both the one-piece and the Princess-line dress block. The skirt section, which hangs from the under-bust seamline, may be straight, tapered or widely flared, the top edge gathered, pleated or smooth. More flare is possible where a centre seam exists. In long dresses, the main design limitation is the width of the fabric to be used which restricts the skirt width.

Left Short Empire-line dress with lace bodice. Follow stage 1 from p51, then draw the new neckline, taking the shoulder seam to just beyond the shoulder point. Slash the skirt from under bust line to hem and spread to required hem width.

Centre Princess Empire-line dress. Use the combined block or the darted strapless block but with less tightening of the midriff area. The shoulder sections can be draped, see p53. The extra skirt seams already allow some hem increase and the panels can be slashed and spread to widen the hem further.

Right The asymmetric design has one fitted sleeve. Outline the bodice blocks to create a whole front and whole back (not just the usual right-hand side). Lower the left armhole by 1cm (⅜") and increase the side seam by 1cm (⅜"). This replaces the necessry tolerance to receive the set in sleeve.

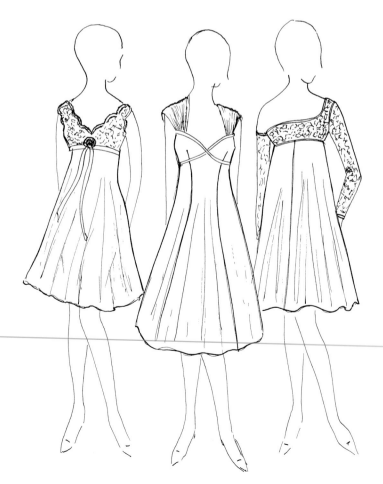

Design note

Horizontal seamlines divide the bodice from the skirt of the dress and open up more
design possibilities.

1 Outline the dress block constructed with the combined bodice. Transfer the shoulder dart into
   the under bust position (by the punctured block method shown for curved darts on p27), then
   continue the line to centre front and centre back.
2 Draw the new neckline and narrow the shoulder seam at the shoulder point
3 A shorter dart can be drawn on the back bodice.
4 Flare the front and back skirts to the required width.

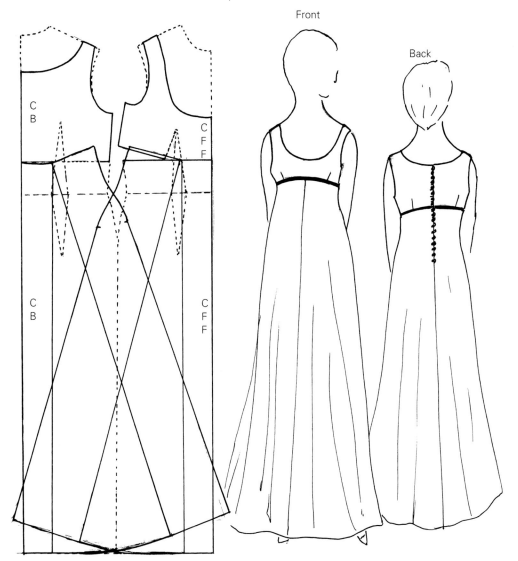

Front

Back

HALTER NECKLINES

Halter necklines extend upwards from a close-fitting, sleeveless bodice and usually fasten at centre back neck. Instructions for constructing the back fastening often follow the back neckline (like a facing) but this does not work well in practice; the 'facing' shape rides up unless kept down by other straps linking it to the back bodice. Without back straps the pattern should be made using the back neckline as the horizontal centre of the strap.

1 Outline the tightened armhole and neckline blocks, pivoting the shoulder dart into the design seam. Add notches.

2 Place the shoulder seam of the back block to touch the front block at the neck point and along the upper part of the shoulder seam. Draw the new neckline, going above the nape in a smooth run over the front bodice to CF. Add CB buttonstand.

3 Draw the lower halter edge from below the nape, across the shoulder, ending at the armhole or side seam, then across to the CB.

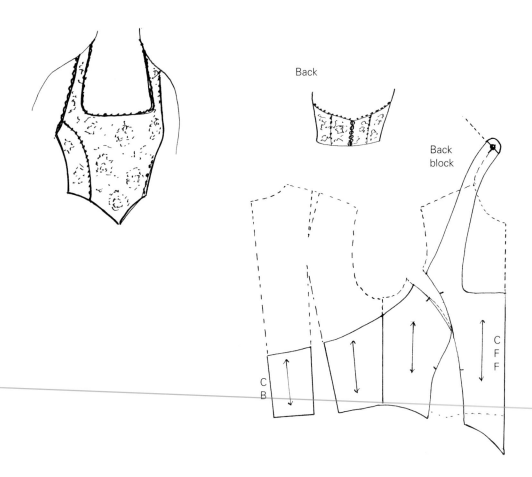

Back

Back block

WORKING ON THE DRESS STAND

It is often simpler and quicker to make the pattern for draped sections of garments by modelling them in fabric directly on the dress stand. The fabric can be coaxed into effective folds, pinned for effect and re-adjusted until satisfactory, all within seconds, without havng to remake the paper pattern. Narrow black tape is used to outline the design seams on the stand as a guide. When the desired effect has been achieved, the fabric is marked along the design lines, notches added and the draped section removed from the stand. Usually, inexpensive fabric, such as calico, is used, then transferred to paper and the marked design lines and notches traced off to produce a paper pattern for future use.

The following pages also illustrate some other ways to achieve the same effect. Most draped sections (or whole bodices, skirts or dresses) need a backing of firm, but lightweight fabric to support the folds. This backing is, essentially, a 'normal'-shaped garment which acts as a lining. The ruched sections are of different sizes and shapes and need to be gathered to fit the lining or modelled independently on the dress stand.

The draped, cross-over top on p54 follows the traditional method of taping the dress stand to indicate the neckline, under-bust band and positions for the folds. The back can also be draped, or a pattern made by flat cutting with paper. In this design, the few folds need no extra support, so a lining would be a matter of choice, not necessity. The neck facing is simply an extension of the fabric, folded under before pinning to the stand.

A different method is used to create the drape on p55. The entire pattern for the dress (not the drape) is made by flat pattern cutting. A simple, strapless dress is shown (the straps are purely decorative and do not support the bodice, which is boned). The front pattern pieces are pinned to the dress stand and a line is drawn on the pattern or a piece of tape pinned over it to indicate the lower edge of the drape. The fabric is then draped over the pattern. This is a very easy way to add draping to an otherwise flat cut pattern.

The ruched panels on p56 again make use of the pattern, which is pinned to the stand. Ruching can be managed by simply cutting a longer piece of fabric and gathering it to fit the basic panel, but it is easier to control the folds when a dress stand is used.

In the example on p57, a dress pattern is made in paper. The centre front bodice is used as a lining, but, pinned to the stand first, becomes the guide for draping the cowl neck shown.

DRAPED CROSSOVER BODICE

For this design, the back may be cut from the block or draped on the stand. Model only the RHS which you can use as a pattern and cut from double material.

1 Pin narrow black tape to the stand to outline the neck and cross the centre front by about 9cm (3"). Tape pleat directions, armhole and bust band width.

2 Cut a piece of fabric on the cross, about 50cm x 50cm (20" x 20"). On the straight grain, mark the front neckline 5cm (2") in from the selvedge for front neck facing. Pin the fold of the neckline to the taped neckline on the stand.

3 Form the top pleat in line with the top tape and pin. Pin the shoulder seam, cut fabric 1cm (⅜") from the seam and start to cut away 1cm (⅜") from the armhole tape. Form the second pleat, smoothing fabric under the arm, pin side seam and smooth across front, cutting and pinning to tape, then pin the third pleat. Cut off surplus fabric. Mark along the upper and inner fold lines. Remove toile from stand and take out pins. Straighten the seamlines and smooth the curves. Trace marked lines on to paper. Mark 'cut two': the pattern is the same for right and left sides.

4 For the under-bust band, cut a strip of X-way fabric for under-bust circumference plus extensions by twice finished depth. Gather at ends and sides in line with side seams.

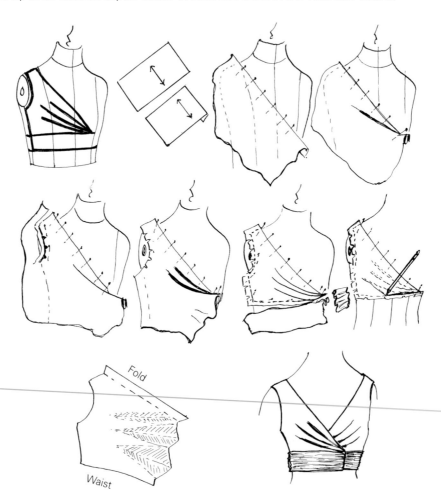

54

DRAPED BODICE FOR STRAPLESS DRESS

This piece of draping is stitched over the bust area before the upper facing is attached.

1   Make the paper pattern for the Princess-line strapless dress. Pin the front of the pattern to the dress stand.

2   Take a piece of fabric, cut on the cross, approximately 60cm x 50cm (23⅝" x 19¾"). Fold the fabric through the centre (widthwise) and run gathering stitches for the centre front.

3   Pin this gathered line to the centre front stand. Holding the remainder of the fabric in the left hand, pull it gently and pin to the side seam. Arrange the folds across the bust and along the upper garment edge and pin. Allow the lower edge to fall naturally in a smooth curve to the side seam. Mark through the gathers on the side seam and the upper edge and pin. Ignore the left-hand side. Remove the draped section from the stand, open out the gathers and join the marks into smooth lines. Cut off surplus fabric. Copy onto paper to make a permanent pattern.

4   Cut off the left-hand-side of the fabric. Only the right hand side is used. Position this onto folded paper (the fold equals the centre front) Trace through the fabric, mark the notches, remove fabric from paper and draw on the traced fitting lines. Mark straight grainline.

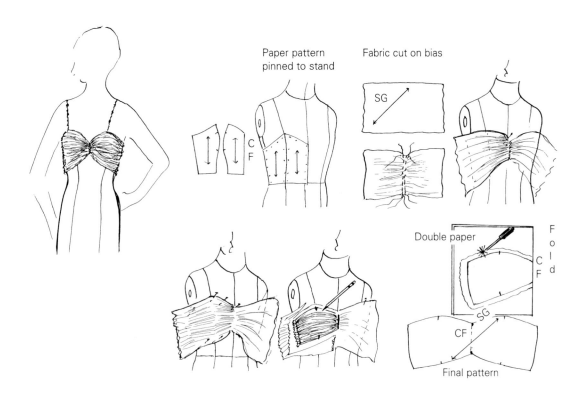

Paper pattern pinned to stand

Fabric cut on bias

Double paper

Final pattern

RUCHED PANELS IN BODICES

1 Make the pattern for the strapless bodice and pin the front panels onto the dress stand. The centre panel pattern will be used to cut the backing for the ruched section.

2 Cut a piece of fabric on the cross for the ruched section. Depending on the fineness of the fabric to be used, the ruched section will be between 2-4 times the length of the original pattern piece but the same width as the pattern.

3 Mark the lengthwise centre of the fabric with fine tacking stitches and gather the outer edges. Pull up the gathers to fit the panel.

4 Bodice (a) Matching the tacked centre to the centre stand seam, pin the ruched panel to the stand, adjusting gathers over the bust area. Pin and mark seamlines to correspond with pattern beneath. Add notches. Remove from stand.

5 Bodice (b) Pull the gathers up tighter on the shorter (underarm) edge, longer on the outer (bust panel seam) edge. Pin to the stand, following the lines of the paper pattern beneath. Mark and complete as for bodice (a).

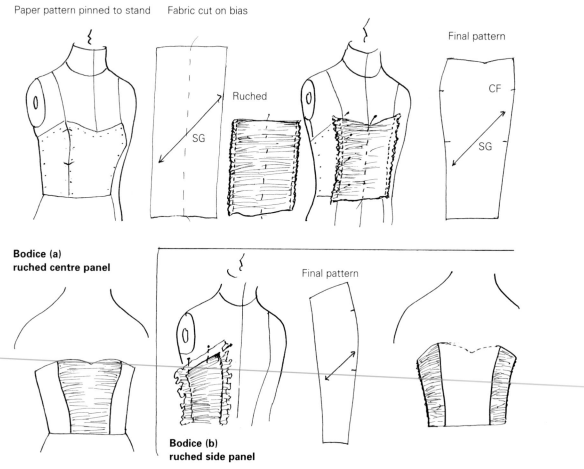

Paper pattern pinned to stand   Fabric cut on bias

Final pattern

Ruched

SG

CF

SG

Bodice (a) ruched centre panel

Final pattern

Bodice (b) ruched side panel

CRINKLE DRAPE DRESS

1 Make the paper pattern, marking notches for the side seam area to be draped, and pin to the stand.

2 Cut the fabric for the front skirt section on the true cross, as long as the fabric will allow. Tack-mark the lengthwise centre of the fabric, align it to the centre front of the pattern on the stand and pin the upper edge. Pin down each side seam to the notches.

3 Working on both side seams simultaneously, gently push the fabric upwards, pinning at very short intervals. The fold will tilt diagonally towards centre front. Stop at the lower notch and pin the remaining side seam in a smooth run.

4 Remove from the stand and use the right hand side to make the pattern.

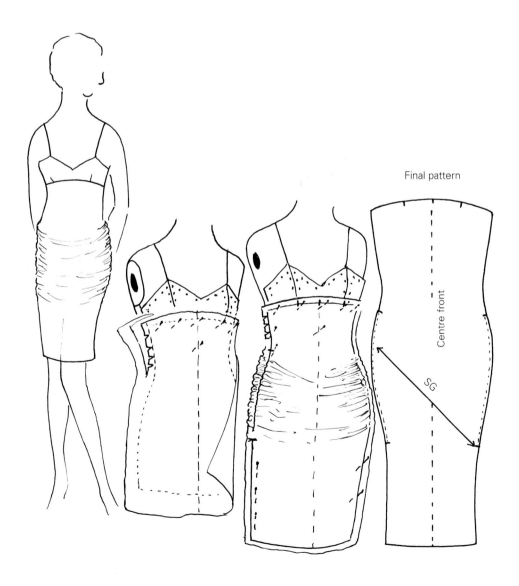

Final pattern

Centre front

SG

COWL NECKLINE

Although only the right-hand-side is used as a basis for making paper patterns (unless the style is asymmetric) it would be impossible to form the folds and achieve the cowl effect without taking the fabric over to the opposite side of the stand. However, it is not necessary to drape both sides. Support the weight of the fabric on the left-hand side of the stand with a few pins and let it form into folds but concentrate on the right-hand side, which will be marked and traced through onto double paper to produce a pattern for the complete cowl section.

1   Make paper pattern for bodice. Pin the front of the pattern to the stand. The centre front panel can be used as a guide for the armhole and neck depth.
2   Cut a piece of X-way fabric about 70cm x 40cm (27½" x 15¾") and tack-mark to centre front.
3   Fold over about 5cm (2") on top edge for front neck facing.
4   Hold each side of the fabric and allow the centre to fall, forming soft folds.
5   Hold the fabric against the dress stand to determine neck depth and pin to shoulders, making sure the tacked centre front still matches the stand centre seamline. Pin the centre front.
6   Mark the shoulder folds. Smooth the remainder of the fabric down and out to the side panel seam, snipping into the fabric to lie flat. Mark seamlines and waist edge and add notches.
7   If calico is used, only the RHS will be used as a pattern. Cut off the LHS. Trace the RHS onto paper to make a pattern.

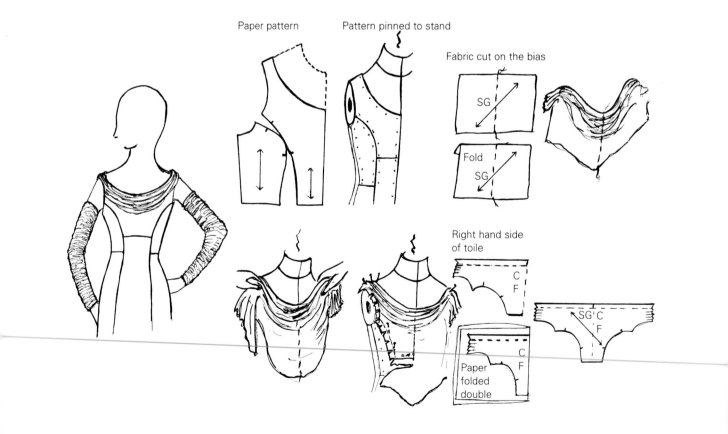

Paper pattern   Pattern pinned to stand

Fabric cut on the bias

SG   Fold   SG

Right hand side of toile

C F   SG' C F   Paper folded double   C F

SHOULDER DRAPES

Shoulder drapes are usually cut from double fabric and seamed to make a tube which is then gathered or pleated. A length of fabric cut on the cross 60cm (23¾") wide, made into a tube and gathered, will produce a drape of approximately 15cm-20cm (6"-8") wide, depending on the fabric thickness. The length depends on the width of the fabric. Find the true cross (the 45 degree angle from selvedge). Fabric of width 112cm-115cm (44"-45") will allow cut length of 90cm-100cm (35"-39").

Measure the shoulders, including the upper arm. Without allowing for stretching, a size 12 requires a minimum of 115cm (over 45") length to encompass the shoulders. Unless a wider fabric is chosen it is rarely possible to cut an entire shoulder drape in one piece. The sketches below show how to overcome this problem. Two lengths of crossway are needed for all the styles and may be cut in various lengths to achieve different effects.

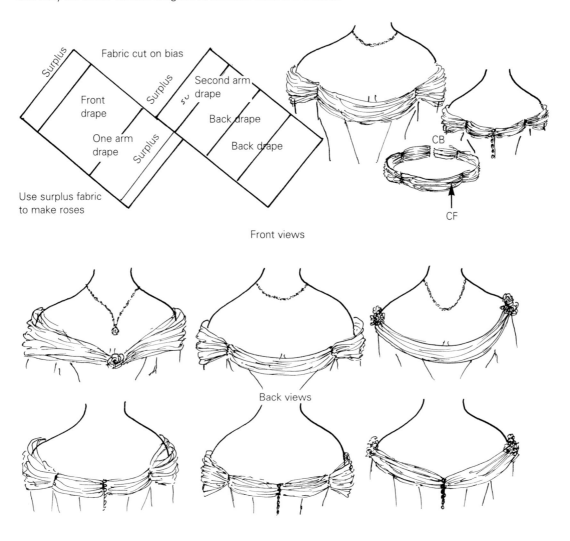

Front views

Back views

SECONDARY SLEEVE BLOCKS

Unless using stretch fabric an opening should be made in long sleeves for the hand to pass through with ease. The traditional position for the opening is on the back line of the sleeve, in line with the elbow and wristbone (see below).

The split French sleeve on p62, however, has the opening in line with the shoulder and in the short sleeve on the same page, the godet is also placed centrally. The two-piece leg o' mutton sleeve on p93 is based on the French sleeve. A diagonal line separates to lower sleeve with its traditional buttoned opening from the lengthened sleevehead, which is widened and more fullness added at crown and lower edge.

Using the block unaltered produces a glove-like fit to the forearm. By cutting off the sleevehead to well above the elbow, a pattern for fingerless gloves or a close fitting separate sleeve is obtained.The upper edge of the separate sleeve needs tightening (usually with elastic) to allow it to grip the arm above the elbow. This pattern can also be used as the backing for the ruched separate sleeves illustrated on p58: follow the directions for ruching on p56, substituting the sleeve for the bodice panel.

FRENCH SLEEVE

The French sleeve is very tight-fitting from above the elbow to the wrist but retains the armhole of the basic bodice block to allow normal arm movement. This secondary block is adapted from the straight sleeve block.

1   Outline the basic straight sleeve block. Reduce underarm seam at wrist by 8cm
    (3") by marking off 4cm (1½") at each side. Redraw lines to underarm
    points.
2   Slash elbow line from back seam to top arm line and from wrist to
    elbow line. Overlap slashed edges at wrist until gap at elbow
    measures 5cm (2"). On elbow line measure half elbow girth plus
    0.5cm (¼") each side.
3   Mark new centre wrist. Measure half wrist measurement plus
    0.5cm (¼") each side. Draw new underarm seam lines from
    underarm point, curving to wrist. Curve wristline. Quarter the
    wristline and mark new back and forearm lines. Add grainline.
4   Final pattern.

French sleeve

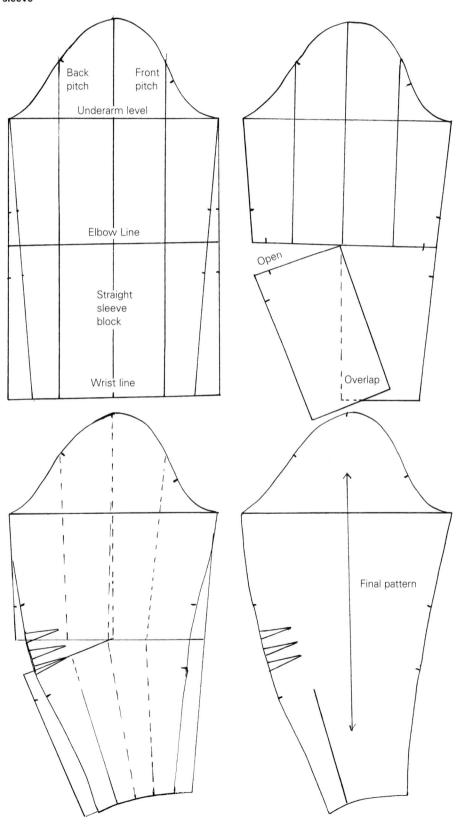

Back pitch

Front pitch

Underarm level

Elbow Line

Straight sleeve block

Wrist line

Open

Overlap

Final pattern

SPLIT FRENCH SLEEVE WITH LOOP AND BUTTON FASTENING

This beautiful sleeve with its finely-bound edges is split to expose the forearm. The button and loop fastening at the ruched wrist is echoed in the single button and loop which controls the upper sleeve.

The sleeve remains in two halves, with an underarm seam. It is not possible to make a one-piece sleeve because of the shape of the wrist. The back and front wrist curves are not identical because the back seam length is longer than the front, with ease at the elbow, to achieve the tight fit.

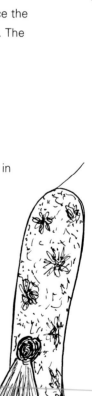

1 Outline French sleeve block. Mark notches.
2 Draw a line from the crown point through the centre of the sleeve, curving gently from mid-forearm to centre wrist. Add notches to indicate the upper buttonloop and the upper and lower ends of the section to be ruched.
3 Draw slash lines for opening out lower sleeve. Trace off lower section and slash on lines to the side seam.
4 Replace on master pattern. Flare outer, slashed edges to approximately twice the original length between notches and redraw the new shape of lower sleeve. The area between the notches will be gathered to the original size.

FRENCH SLEEVE WITH GODET

The godet is a device for allowing body movement and is found more frequently in skirts than in sleeves. Here, the godet allows the elbow to move freely in an otherwise tight-fitting short sleeve.

1 Outline the French sleeve block. Add notches. Shorten to required length.
2 Draw a line through the centre from crown point to new lower edge. Trace off and cut sleeve apart.
3 Replace on master pattern, opening out at the sleevehead to increase the top width. To increase the height, raise the crown point and redraw the sleevehead in a smooth curve.
4 Mark an opening in the centre of the lower sleeve edge. Draw a circle where the diameter is the length of the opening. Cut from the outer edge to the centre. The cut edges are the same length as the opening.

Slashed French sleeve

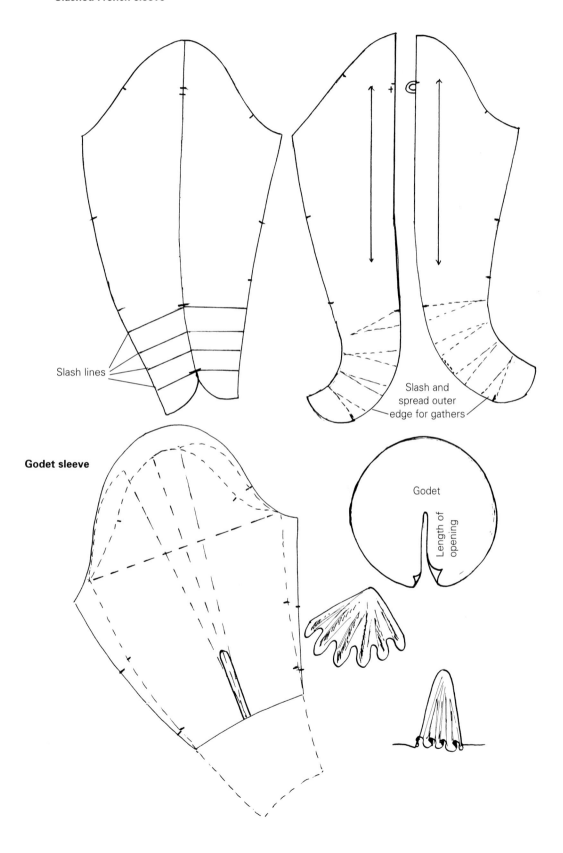

Slash lines

Slash and
spread outer
edge for gathers

Godet sleeve

Godet

Length of
opening

TIERED PETAL SLEEVE

The single layer petal sleeve (1) on p65 appears to be in two parts, but is a one-piece sleeve; there is no underarm seam. It may be cut from the straight or the fitted sleeve block. The long outer edge of the final pattern (1b) is the hem and should be neatened before overlapping the front sleeve over the back.

Petal sleeves have curved hems which need careful neatening. In a single layer sleeve a lining can be used, stitched only to the hem edge and pressed to the inside. The sleeve and lining of the armhole edge are tacked together before overlapping and machining into the armhole. The sleeve cap can be given more height and gathers introduced. If a smooth finish is preferred, surplus ease in the sleeve cap caused by raising its height can be collected in a dart centred to match the shoulder seam of the garment.

The only limitation on the number of tiers is the bulk created in the armhole seam, so only fine, soft fabrics should be considered. The outer hems can be overlocked, narrowly machined or hand rolled.

[for a]
1   Outline the sleeve block to the length required; mark the crown notch.
2   Draw on the design lines and mark the straight grainlines parallel to sleeve centre. Mark 'back' on the left and 'front' on the right.

[for b]
1   Trace off each side separately, replace the back half sleeve next to the front at the underarm seam and mark with a notch.

Three tiered sleeve

The second sleeve (2) has three tiers and 2a illustrates the flaring of slash lines to obtain a wider sleeve hem, after which the three tiers are drawn (2b)

Trace off the sections for each layer, as in the previous sleeve, to create three separate sleeves of different lengths.

2c shows the further flaring in the overarm hem edge area only, to add more hem width. It is also possible to gather the sleevehead if very fine fabric is used.

Petal sleeves

[a] Straight petal sleeve

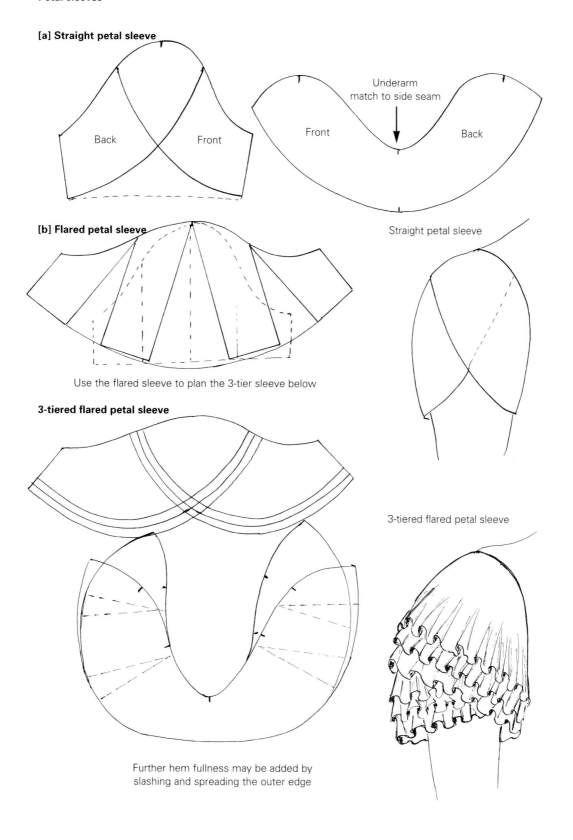

Back Front

Front Back

Underarm
match to side seam

Straight petal sleeve

[b] Flared petal sleeve

Use the flared sleeve to plan the 3-tier sleeve below

3-tiered flared petal sleeve

3-tiered flared petal sleeve

Further hem fullness may be added by
slashing and spreading the outer edge

SECONDARY SKIRT BLOCKS

FISHTAIL SKIRT

This is an interesting device for widening the hem of a closely-fitting skirt or dress without destroying the silhouette. The extra fabric falls from a point high enough to allow knee movement and freedom for the legs and feet for dancing. In long skirts, fishtails are a dramatic design statement. In shorter skirts they are considerably modified.

ANKLE-LENGTH SKIRT WITH FLARED FISHTAIL

1   Outline the basic block, extend it to ankle length and add darts and notches. Taper the side seams inwards in a smooth curve from just below the hipline through knee level, then straight to the hem.
2   Add flare at sides and centre back (which may be lengthened to drag on the floor). Draw the diagonal design line from centre front to the front side seam, then from the same horizontal point on the back side seam to the centre back. Add notches. Draw slash lines from this line to the hem.
3   Cut off the lower skirt section, slash the lines without breaking them at the top. Spread the lower edge out to the fullness required. The only limitation is the fabric width.
4   For a gathered fishtail (shown below), cut the lower sections apart on the slash lines and spread them out to the required width.

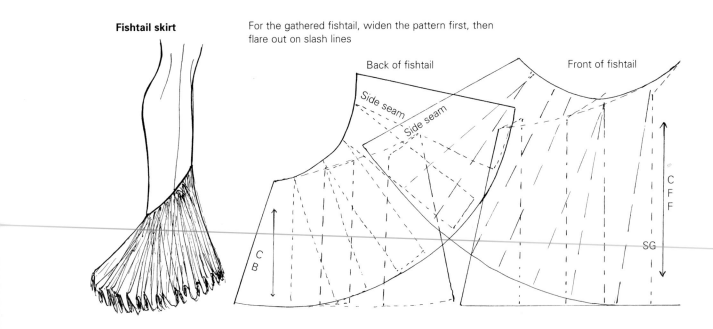

Fishtail skirt

For the gathered fishtail, widen the pattern first, then flare out on slash lines

Back of fishtail

Front of fishtail

Side seam

Side seam

C B

C F F

SG

Flared fishtail

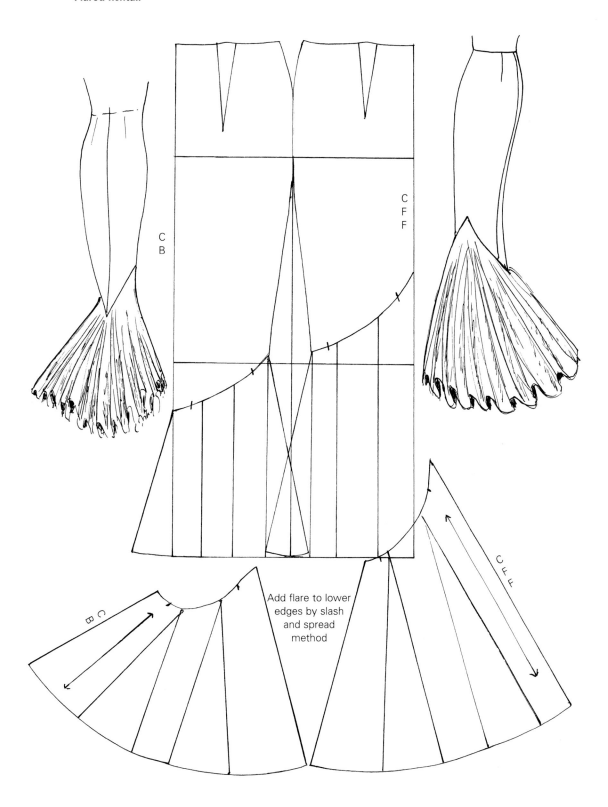

Add flare to lower
edges by slash
and spread
method

THE GODET

The godet is an extra piece of fabric inserted into a seam or slash in the garment to create extra walking room. There may be one only in a skirt, or many; they may fall from the knee or higher, and the longer the opening into which they are stitched, the more material is introduced and hem fullness increased.

1   Mark the point from which the godet will fall, either on a seamline or as a slash. Measure from this point to the hem. eg, 50cm (19¾").
2   Draw a semi-circle with a radius of 50cm (19¾"). The diameter will be 100cm (39⅜"). Mark a notch at 50cm (19¾").
3   The longer edge is the stitching line from skirt hem to the point measured on the skirt and its return to the hem. The notch marks the point of return.

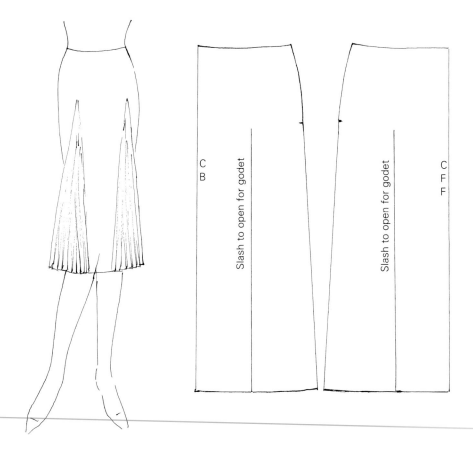

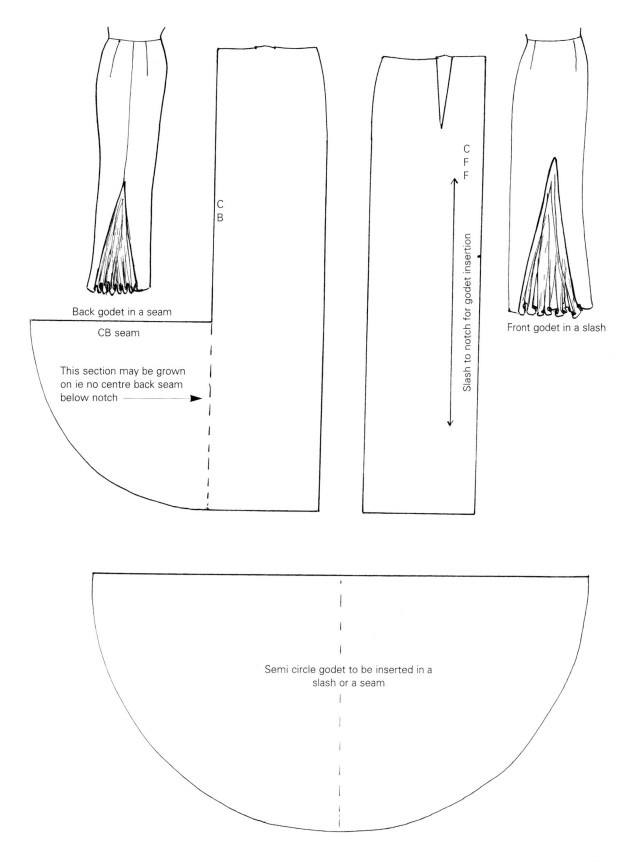

Back godet in a seam

CB seam

This section may be grown
on ie no centre back seam
below notch ⟶

C
B

C
F
F

Slash to notch for godet insertion

Front godet in a slash

Semi circle godet to be inserted in a
slash or a seam

WRAPOVER SKIRT

This skirt is a classic and has many variations from straight to full and comes in all lengths. It is very effective as a separate skirt in satin or velvet, worn with a contrast top, or in the guise of a dress with a separate matching bodice, often including a peplum, giving the effect of a jacket and skirt.

1 Outline the back and front skirt blocks, flipping the front block over to obtain the left side. This is an asymmetric style.

2 Taper the side seams and draw on the wrapover design line. The dart positions may be moved over so the the one on the left-hand side will be hidden beneath the right wrap when closed. The dart control may also be used as a tuck.

3 Trace off the back skirt and only the right hand side front skirt, which will be cut from double fabric.

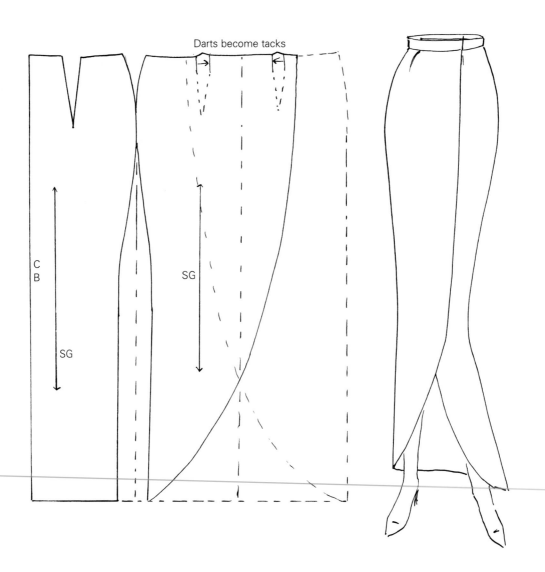

Darts become tacks

FULL SKIRT ON BODICE

This strapless dress with lowered, shaped waistline and fully gathered skirt may be cut to any length from a 'ballerina' mini-skirt to full length. Use the dress block with fully contoured strapless, panel line bodice.

1 Outline the blocks and draw on the lowered waistline.
2 Draw on flare lines as shown for the Princess-line dress on p49. Add notches and grainlines.
3 Trace off the skirt panels separately, slash the flare lines and spread apart to widen the panels to double their width from upper edge to hem.

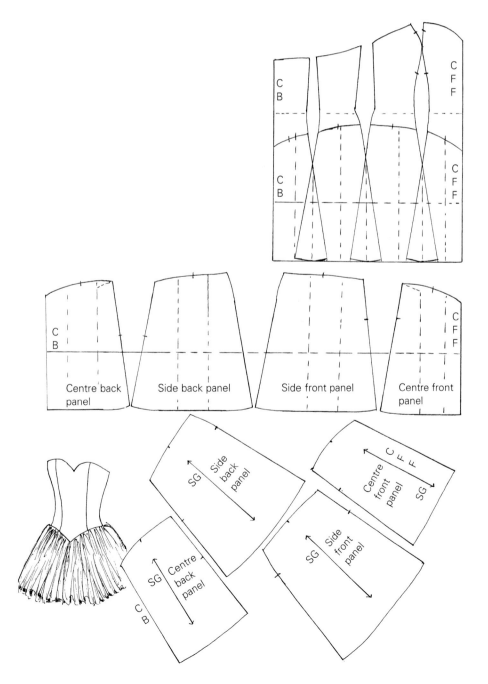

SECONDARY JACKET BLOCKS

JACKET BLOCK ADAPTED FROM DRESS BODICE BLOCK

Draw round the back and front hip-length bodice blocks with the CB and CF lines parallel, leaving a space between the blocks for widening the side seams.

BACK

1. Raise neckline 0.5cm (¼"). Raise SP 0.5cm (¼"). Draw the new shoulder seam and extend it by 0.5cm (¼"). Draw new neckline from new NP to CB.
2. Add 0.5cm (¼") to the back width armhole at XB level. Lower UP 1cm (⅜"). For semi-fitted or loose styles, widen by 0.5cm-1cm (¼"-⅜").
3. Move UP and W out 0.5cm (¼") and side hip out and down 0.5cm (¼").
4. Draw the new armhole. Draw the new hipline from CB to side seam.
5. Redraw underam side seam on the line or just outside it, curving in 0.5cm (¼") at waist level if a closer fit is required, and down to the new hip level.
6. On CB, for a slanted seam, narrow the waist by 1cm-1.5cm (⅜"-⅝"). Redraw CB line.

FRONT

7. Move NP 0.5cm (¼") outwards to widen neck and raise it 0.5cm (¼"). Raise SP 0.5cm (¼") and move it out 0.5cm (¼") to lengthen the shoulder.
8. Reduce shoulder dart by 0.5cm (¼") on side nearest neck and move lower point of shoulder dart 0.5cm (¼") towards CF and 1.5cm-2cm (⅜"-¾") up to shorten the dart. Redraw the dart legs.
9. Pin the new dart closed and redraw the shoulder seam between the new NP and SP.
10. Add 0.5cm (¼") at the front pitch and redraw the armhole. Move hip point out and down 0.5cm (¼") to match back. Redraw the side underarm seam to match back.
11. Mark a point 0.5cm (¼") outside the CF waist and rule a new CF line from the base of neck through this point to 1.3cm (½") below the hipline. This adds 1cm (⅜") to the hips. Connect to the side seam.
12. Redraw neckline.

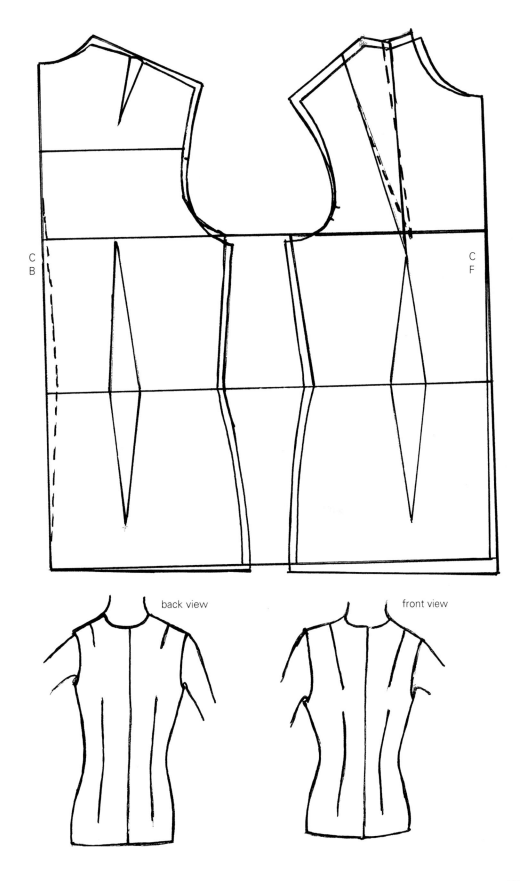

C
B

C
F

back view

front view

JACKET SLEEVE BLOCK

The dress bodice block needs to be widened and lengthened to produce a jacket large enough to go over normal daywear. The jacket sleeve must have corresponding increases in order to fit the jacket armhole. The instructions show the alterations made to the straight sleeve block. From this, semi-fitted and fitted sleeves can be developed.

The straight jacket sleeve is a good basis for jacket and coat sleeves for evening and partywear where sleeves are more often widened than narrowed, in order to go over elaborate sleeves of dresses.

1   Lightly outline the dress straight sleeve block. Mark the centre line and the elbow line.
2   Lower UP by 1cm (½") and widen by 0.5cm (¼") to the wristline. Widen sides of sleevehead by 0.5cm (¼") and raise CP 0.5cm (¼"). Join to make new outer sleevehead seamline.
3   Fold or mark the sleeve into four vertical columns and mark new pitch points 1cm (½") above those of the dress block to compensate for moving the underarm line down 1cm (½"). Mark forearm, back and centre lines, underarm, elbow and wristlines and elbow point.

SLEEVEHEAD ANALYSIS

When changes are made to block outlines during the construction stages of pattern making, the sleevehead circumference changes size and needs to be checked against the circumference of the armhole. The amount of ease to be left in the sleeve cap for the correct insertion of the sleeve into the armhole also needs consideration. Natural fibres can be eased or shrunk to fit and several centimetres of ease can be absorbed. Synthetic fibres are less easy to manipulate and it is difficult to ease more than 1.5cm-2cm (⅝"-¾") into the upper armhole. The diagrams below indicate how to assess the surplus in the cap of the sleeve.

Check the circumferences of back and front jacket block armhole.
Check the circumferences of front and back jacket sleeve armholes.
Make sure the sleeve block is a minimum of 1.5cm (⅝") larger than the jacket armhole.
Check that front and back pitch marks match on bodice and sleeve and adjust if necessary.

> **Design note**
> A balance must be kept between the crown height of the sleeve and the height of the jacket bodice above the underarm. If the sleevehead is already more than about 14cm (5½"), consider extending the underarm line to add extra sleevehead length rather than raising the crown height unduly.

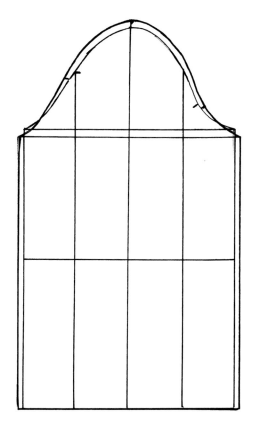

Inner continuous line = straight sleeve of dress block
Outer continuous line = sleeve block

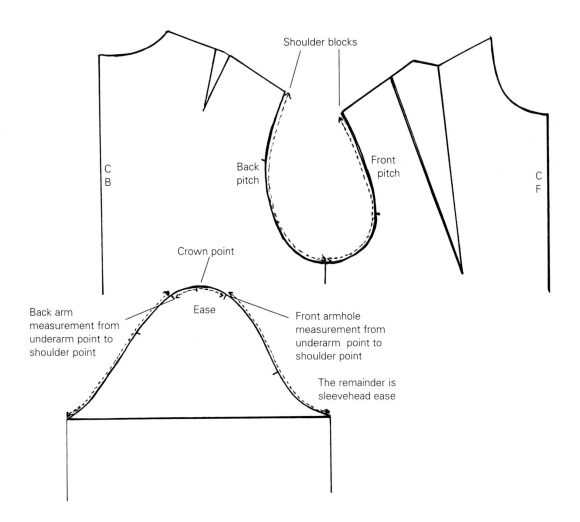

Shoulder blocks

C
B

Back
pitch

Front
pitch

C
F

Crown point

Back arm
measurement from
underarm point to
shoulder point

Ease

Front armhole
measurement from
underarm point to
shoulder point

The remainder is
sleevehead ease

The jacket blocks produced from the basic blocks are not tailoring blocks, but dressmaker blocks. Tailoring involves a different method of producing patterns, a technique called drafting, based on direct measurements. The draft reflects the techniques used in the making up of tailored garments, including shaping by stretching and shrinking with the iron and steam, padding, stay tapes and other methods used to preserve the shape in wear. These are techniques suitable for traditional tailoring fabics and are used mainly for outdoor garments. The softer nature of dressmaking fabric does not lend itself well to the firmer look of tailoring and relies more on darts and seams for shaping a close fit.

The jacket block developed from the dress bodice block is therefore more suitable for a designer suit in silk, linen or fine wool: the couturier look.

These patterns are suitable for use with most dressmaking fabrics and they require the following techniques:

1   The use of darts and panel lines to suppress or control surplus fabric.
2   The inclusion of body tolerance (extra room for body movement within the garment).
3   Ease (extra fabric for specific purposes, such as fitting a sleevehead into an armhole to give a smooth, rounded finish).
4   Manipulating garment silhouette in ways suitable for the construction techniques applicable to these light weight fabrics. Features such as fishtails, used to increase hem width and change the silhouette, could only apply to dressmaker fabrics.

The jacket block can be extended to any length, even to floor length, but it has only enough tolerance for a jacket or coat to wear over a dress. It would require further adjustment to be worn over thick garments.

The front shoulder dart, like that of the bodice and dress blocks, is rarely used as a design feature. It is a device to control the necessary suppression of fabric in the narrower areas of the body. It can be manipulated into other positions or design seams and used to create flare in the same way as the darts of bodice and dress blocks.

Coats for special occasionwear are designed to go over a variety of skirt shapes. The coat on p90 is developed from the extended jacket block and has a flared skirt.

JACKET PEPLUMS

1 Outline jacket block, pivoting shoulder dart into a curved side seam panel.

2 Add buttonstand and curve lower front edge to side seam. Add notches and grainlines.

3 Add flare to side seam and darts from the waistline.

1 Outline jacket blocks. Add buttonstand and curve to side seam. Add flare to the side seam and the back dart.

2 For the double pleat add four times the width of one pleat from centre back seamline. Mark back waist belt. Add notches and grainlines.

3 Trace off the peplum. Close out the darts to create flare. This may be increased by further spreading.

Peplum created by flared princess seams

Princess-line jacket with grown-on peplum

Waisted jacket with separate peplum

SECONDARY TROUSER BLOCKS

The trouser block is another secondary block and is developed from the upper part of the skirt block. Refer to the size chart for measurements.

1   Draw a horizontal line across the paper. Outline the top of the skirt blocks to hip level on this line. Move the centre back waist point up by 2cm (¾") and inwards by 2cm (¾").
2   Draw crotch level (body rise measurement) 29cm (11⅜") below front waistline and parallel with hipline, extending it beyond centre back and centre front.
3   Mark front fork out from centre front on crotchline as one-tenth of the hip measure minus 1cm (⅜") eg: For size 12: 94cm (37") divided by 10 = 9.4cm (3¾"). Take off 1cm (⅜") to make 8.4cm (3¼") and round up to 8.5cm (3⅜").
4   To obtain back fork point measure back along the crotchline from the front forkpoint as 75 per cent of the hip measurement minus 2.5cm (1").
    eg For size 12: 75 per cent of the hip measurement of 94cm (37") = 70.5cm (27¾"). Take off 2.5cm (1") to make 68cm (26¾").
5   To establish side seam length rule a vertical line 100cm (39⅜") from side waist point to ankle. Rule across paper, parallel to crutch line.
6   Rule knee line 58cm (22⅞") from side waist point. Rule across paper.
7   Draw crotch curve from just above hipline on centre front to front forkpoint through a point 4cm (1⅝") from the angle of centre front and crotchline.
8   Drop the back fork 1.3cm (½"). Draw back crotch curve to this point.

Waistband

1   Crease lines and hide seams. Here, two small darts of 2cm (¾") each have been drawn on both back and front blocks and 0.5cm (¼") taken off each side seam. For convenience, one of the darts on front and back are positioned at the top of the crease lines, although they may be moved elsewhere, according to the design. The darts should be kept quite short, coming to or just below the high hip line. Waistbands usually fasten at centre back or at the left-hand side.

2   Draw waistband the exact waist size and double the width required, usually between 2.5cm-5cm (1"-2"), plus an underwrap of 4cm (1½"). Mark foldline through centre. Add notches to indicate matching points to waistline at side seams, CF and CB.

Seam pocket

1   Mark the pocket opening on the side seams, long enough to insert a hand.

2   Draw the pocket bag from the waistband to well below the opening. The grainline is parallel to the centre front trouser. The back and front of the pocket are the same size and shape.

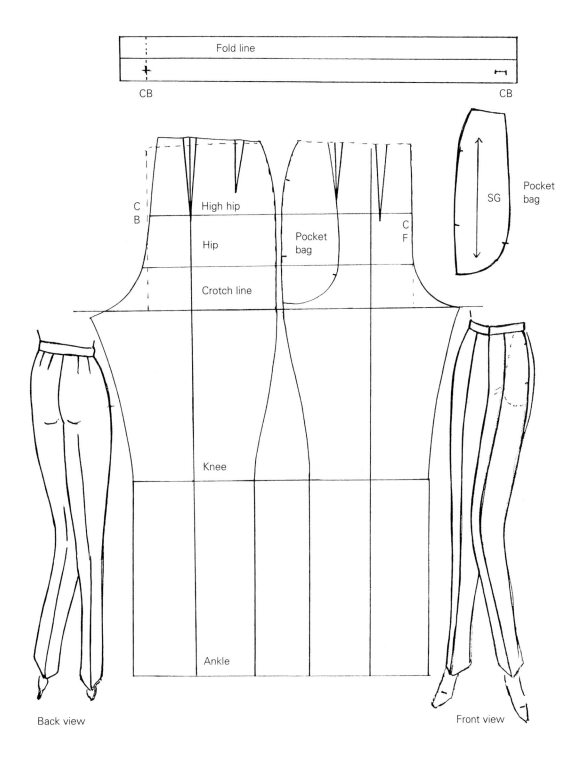

Fold line

CB

CB

C
B

High hip

Hip

Pocket
bag

Crotch line

C
F

SG

Pocket
bag

Knee

Ankle

Back view

Front view

TROUSERS WITH RAISED WAISTLINE AND TAPERED WAIST .

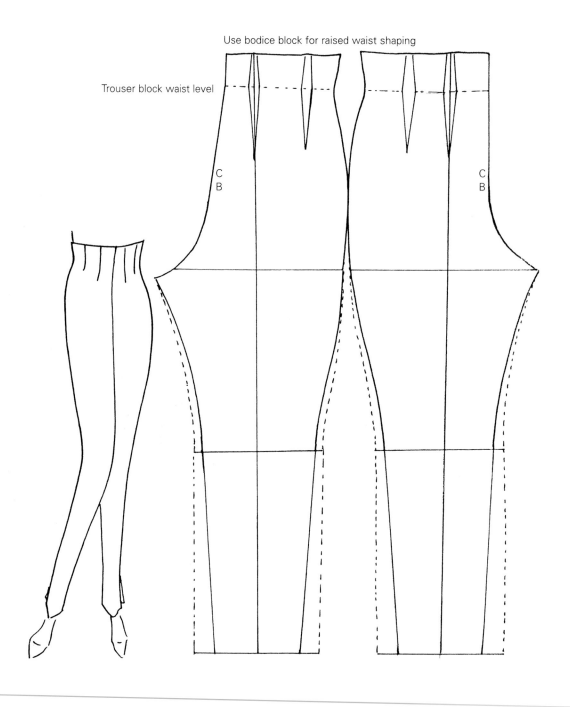

Use bodice block for raised waist shaping

Trouser block waist level

C B

C B

HIPSTERS

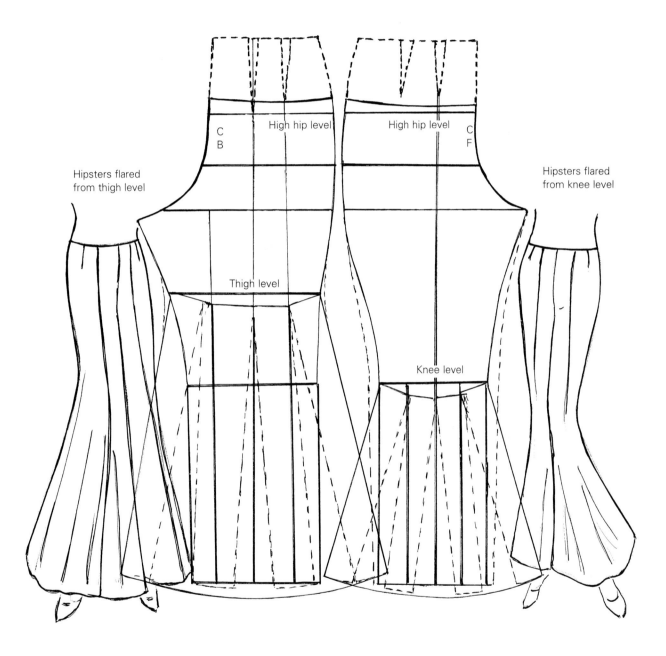

TROUSERS WITH RAISED WAISTBAND

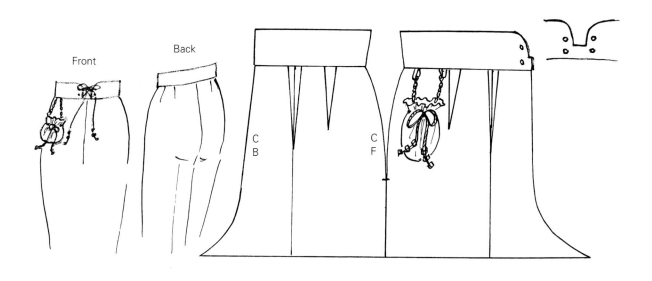

YOKED TROUSERS

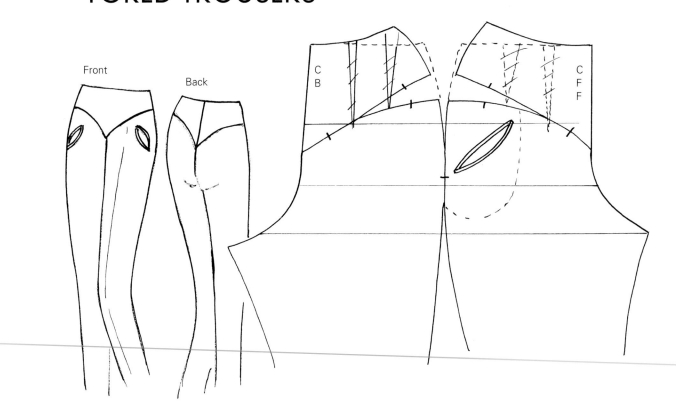

WRAPFRONT TROUSERS

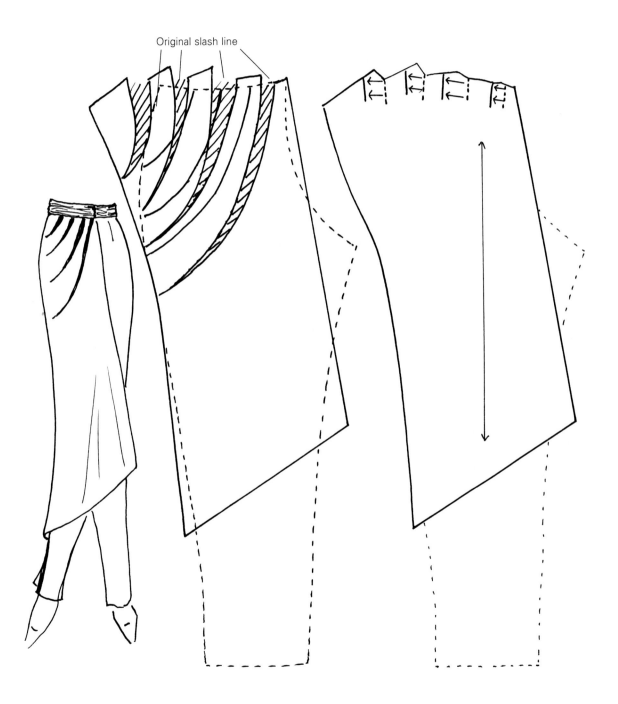

Original slash line

SECONDARY STRETCH BLOCKS

Basic blocks include extra room for body tolerance. The secondary blocks for close fit discussed so far have reduced body tolerance to the minimum required when working with woven fabrics. Stretch fabrics require even further reduction, to body size and less, according to the degree of 'stretch and recovery' in the fabric to be used. The following blocks are suitable for tops, trousers, skirts and dresses with a little 'cling' in fabrics such as stretch velvet, satin, lace and brocade.

STRETCH DRESS BLOCK

The bodice is prepared first, then the skirt added, as in the one-piece dress block.

1   Outline the basic bodice block, pivoting the shoulder dart into the side seam, level with the bust line.
2   Shorten the front bodice by measuring half the bust dart width and draw a line to centre front. Fold out this strip to shorten the neck to waist measurement. The remainder of the dart becomes ease. Add notches to back and front side seams.
3   To narrow the block draw a line from mid shoulder to waist, parallel to the centre front. Mark points 0.5cm (¼") at the shoulder from this line and 3cm (1⅛") from this line at the waist. Connect the points and remove this section. This removes approximately 1.5cm (⅝") across the bust. Mark in 0.5cm (¼") at underarm points and draw a new side seam to normal waist. The block is now narrowed by 2cm (¾") from armhole to waist.
4   To shorten the bodice neckline and armhole mark a new neckpoint 0.3cm (⅛") down and new shoulder point 0.5cm (¼") down on both back and front blocks. Connect points for new shoulder seams.

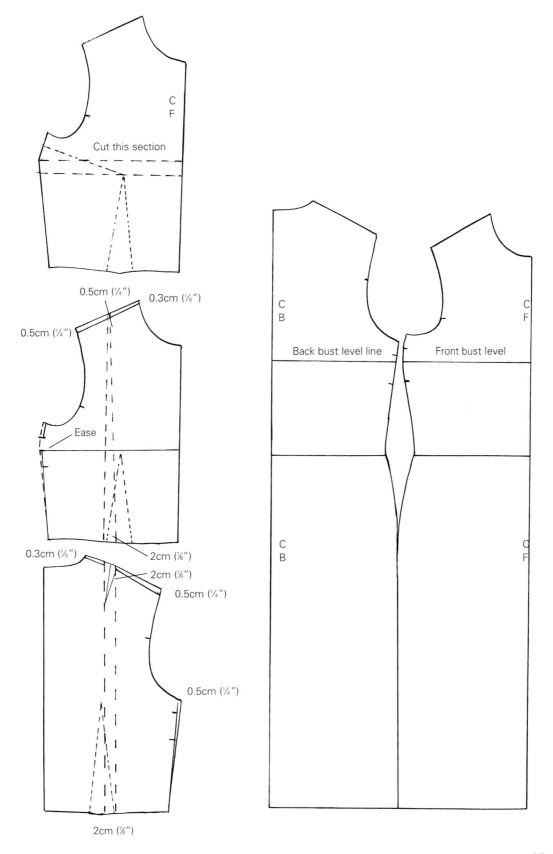

Cut this section

C
F

0.5cm (¼")

0.5cm (¼")   0.3cm (⅛")

Ease

0.3cm (⅛")   2cm (⅞")

2cm (⅞")

2cm (⅞")

0.5cm (¼")

0.5cm (¼")

2cm (⅞")

C
B

C
F

Back bust level line   Front bust level

C
B

C
F

STRETCH SLEEVE BLOCK

1 Use the French sleeve block and take in both sides by 0.5cm (¼″) from the underarm point through elbow to wrist.

2 Shorten the sleevehead by taking a tuck 0.5cm (¼″) across the sleeve cap.

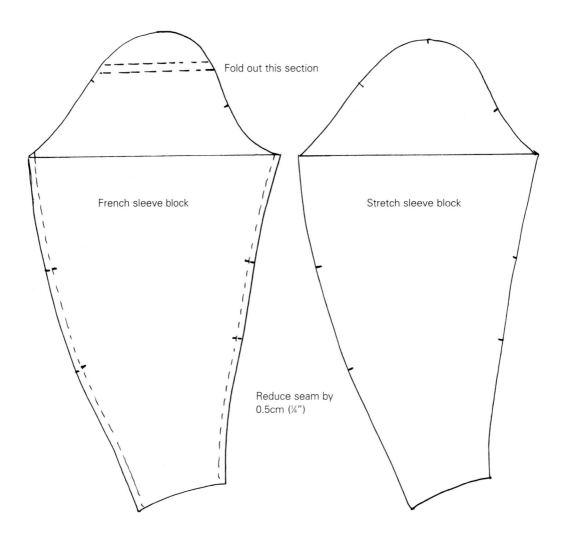

Fold out this section

French sleeve block

Stretch sleeve block

Reduce seam by 0.5cm (¼″)

STRETCH TROUSERS BLOCK

The trousers block is narrowed in two places: from waist to ankle and from crotch to ankle. These sections can be removed by tucks or cutting and overlapping, or simply by outlining the block outer (side) seam 1.5cm (⅝") inside the original and redrawing the block inner leg seam inside the original. Check that no seam length has been lost.

Reduce side seams 1.5cm (⅝") then by amount of remaining darts

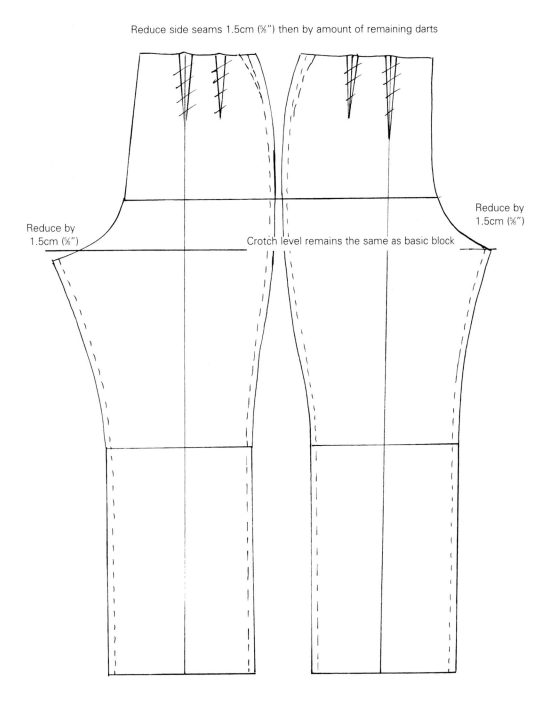

Reduce by 1.5cm (⅝")

Reduce by 1.5cm (⅝")

Crotch level remains the same as basic block

STRETCH EVENING DRESS

The stretch dress block may be divided at the waist and used separately for bodices and skirts. The small amount of body tolerance remaining in the bodice can be eased into the seamed waistline of a dress and the same amount of tolerance in a skirt can be eased into a waistband.

The stretch block may be used in conjunction with any of the other blocks in the same garment. It is the fabric which dictates the choice of a stretch or a non-stretch block. When combining stretch and non-stretch fabrics in the same garment, remember to allow the necessary body tolerance for the non-stretch fabrics. Stretch fabric in the bodice is effective when combined with non-stretch fabric in the skirt and sleeves (see p89). When lace is used, it is most effective when seams can be eliminated, so that the lace motifs remain unbroken. The dress bodice opposite has no seams (except the centre back opening). Instead of side seams, a small, inconspicuous dart under the arm allows the bust tolerance in the front bodice to be eased into the back bodice, so a beautiful embroidered or lac e fabric can remain uncut.

1   Outline stretch bodice blocks with lower side seams touching, leaving a dart shape gap between the bodice arm holes. (This will be stitched as a dart and includes the bust tolerance)

2   Draw the off the shoulder neckline and continues across the gap between the bodice armholes. Notch the centre of the band for the top arm, underarm dart, and the under bust seam line (for joining to skirt). Mark CF fold. Trace off the bodice and cut out the armholes.

3   The skirt is a length of fabric cut on the straight grain to the length required. The width may be between 2-3 or more times the measurement of the under bust seam , depending on the fabric width being used. Joins may be needed for a very full skirt but a border fabric may be cut in one piece.

4   For the sleeve, trace the sleeve block; its cap will be removed. Measure the height from the underarm level on the back bodice t the lower edge of thearm strap and remove this amount form the sleeve head.

5   Draw the curved line for the lower part of the sleeve. Mark the sleeve opening. Trace off this back section of the sleeve and transfer it to the front side, thereby eliminating an uneccessary seam. Add a narrow buttonstand fo thte buttons. Add grain line.

6   Add length to the upper sleeve by a curved line dipping 10cm (4") below the lower arm section. Notch the seamline. Trace off the upper sleeve. Cut and spread it to the required width for gathers. Add grainline.

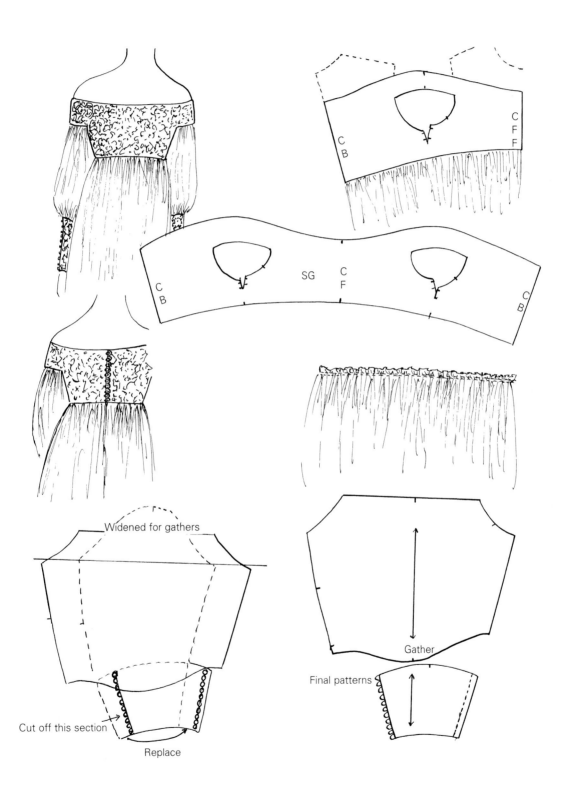

Widened for gathers

Cut off this section

Replace

Gather

Final patterns

CAPSULE WARDROBE

A few well-chosen garments can answer for a variety of special occasions, particularly if they are interchangeable. Try planning your own collection from the variety of bodices, skirts, trousers and jackets shown. Choose complementary design lines and a colour theme for the main garments, a 'capsule wardrobe', to which you can add dramatic touches. Dress it up or down with accessories as the occasion requires and introduce other garments from time to time to make a special statement, such as a stunning pair of velvet trousers, a bright silk blouse or a beaded camisole.

It is easier to achieve different looks with a few well-cut skirts and trousers if you keep to a colour scheme and classic lines. A wardrobe of garments that don't go together can be a hindrance; it is better to possess a few toning skirts and jackets that can be dresssed up with a touch of colour in a stunning top or a piece of jewellery. Classic shapes, uncluttered by unnecessary detail, may sound unimaginative, but it is against such a background that dramatic touches are most effective and individual. The ability to design clothes, make patterns and assemble garments allows the choice of the best quality fabrics and trimmings.

ANKLE-LENGTH EVENING COAT

This coat is designed to go over a party or evening dress and may be constructed from the lengthened jacket block. If a roomier coat is required, the block may be further widened the same way as the jacket block was developed from the dress block.

1   Outline the jacket block, extend to the required length and transfer the shoulder dart into the side seam using the curved dart method (p27). In this instance the curve was drawn on the block to coincide with the design lines and punched through before pivoting.
2   Lower the neckline 2cm-3cm (¾"-1⅛") and draw on the yoke lines about 4cm (1⅝") apart from front neckline to centre back.
3   Add flare lines to the skirt, then trace off skirt and curved yoke inset. Flare the skirt to the required width. Fold out the remaining darts in the yoke band. Replace both on the master pattern and redraw.
4   For the collar, measure the lowered neckline and divide this width by two. Draw a rectangle this length by the collar depth. Mark centre back and centre front and curve the front edge. Mark the new neckpoint on the lower (neck) edge of collar: measure equals centre back neckline to neckpoint on coat.
5   For the sleeve, outline the jacket sleeve block, pivoting it to the left and right to increase the width at wrist and sleevehead. Recurve the sleeve cap, raising the crown point a fraction. Draw the new wrist shape and repeat the same width band as in the bodice.

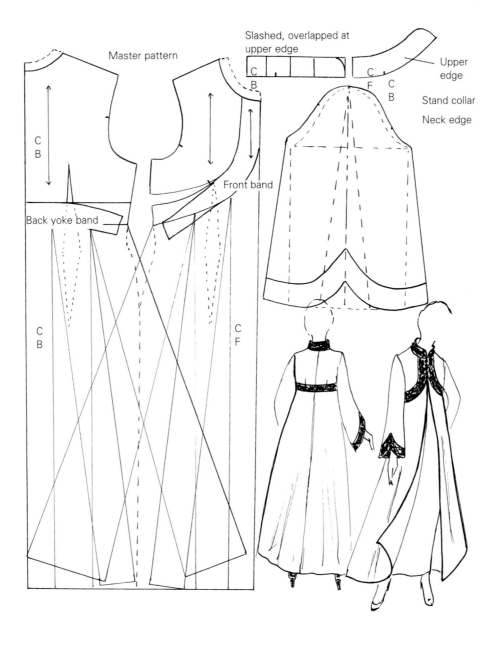

Master pattern

Slashed, overlapped at
upper edge

C
B

C
B

Upper
edge

C
F
C
B

Stand collar

Neck edge

C
B

Front band

Back yoke band

C
B

C
F

Necklines

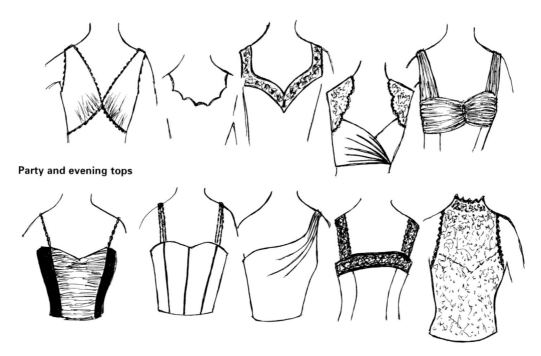

Party and evening tops

Trousers

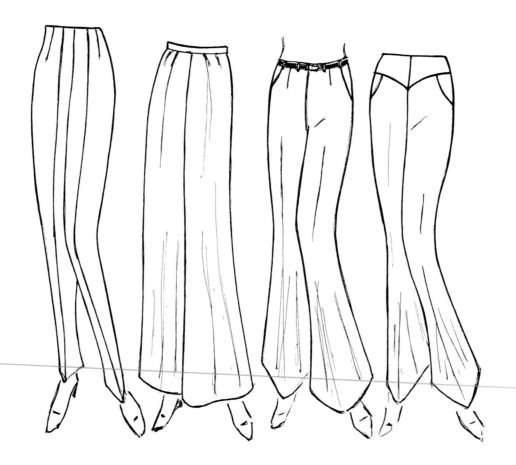

Jackets

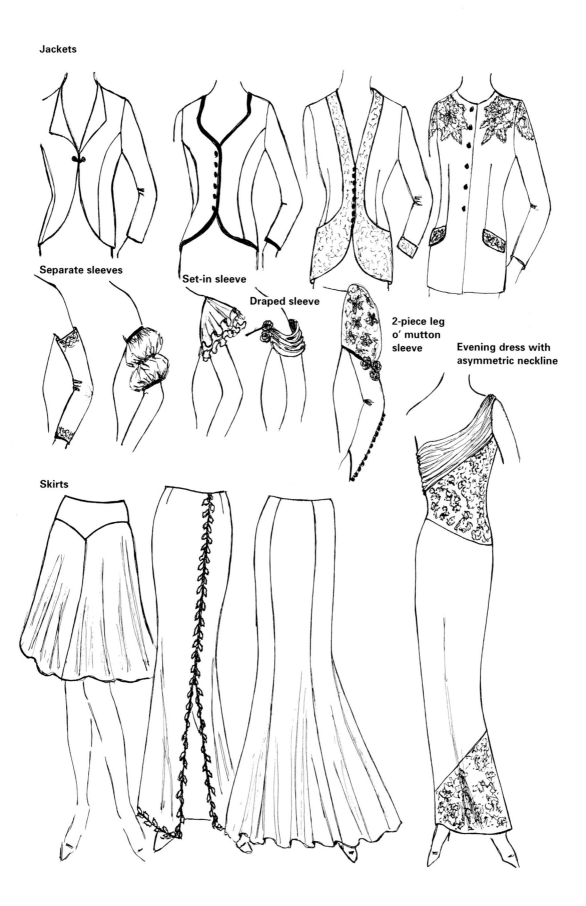

Separate sleeves

Set-in sleeve

Draped sleeve

2-piece leg o' mutton sleeve

Evening dress with asymmetric neckline

Skirts

GLOSSARY

block

basic pattern constructed from body measurements plus tolerance for movement

body tolerance

extra measurement added to body measurement to allow normal body movement

bias

cut across the diagonal of the fabric at an angle of 45 degrees

bustier

close-fitting bodice with visible stitching of the bone insertion

contoured block

bodice block for very tight fitting garments

dart manipulation

ways of changing the dart to other positions or into seams

draping

creating intricate folds – 'drapes' – by manipulating fabric on the dress stand

Empire line

horizontal design line under the bust, dividing bodice from skirt

flare

a widening of fabric from a narrow part

French sleeve

a very tight fitting sleeve but with a normal armhole fit

girth

measurement all round a part of the body: bust, waist, hip

modelling

shaping fabric on the dress stand, not necessarily draping

pivoting

a method of changing dart positions

princess line

vertical design lines passing through the waistline

ruching

gathered fabric enclosed between seams

secondary block

a more advanced block developed from the basic block

shell

a commercial pattern similar to a block

slash and spread

a method of changing dart positions by cutting and spreading

sleeveless block

block with tightened armhole for sleeveless styles

toile

trial garment made from a pattern or modelled on dress stand

SUPPLIERS LIST

FABRICS AND HABERDASHERY

MacCullock and Wallis Ltd.
25–26 Dering Street
London, W1R 0BH
www.macculloch-wallis.co.uk

John Lewis
300 Oxford Street
London, W1C 1DX
www.johnlewis.com

Whaleys Bradford Ltd.
Harris Court
Great Horton
Bradford
West Yorkshire, BD7 4EQ
www.whaleys-bradford.ltd.uk

James Hare Silks
Monarch House
Queen Street
Leeds, LS1 2TW
www.james-hare.com

DRESS STANDS

Kennett and Lindsell Ltd.
Crow Lane, Romford
Essex, RM7 0ES
www.kennettlindsell.com

BOOKS AND SUPPLIERS

Morplan
56 Great Titchfield Street
London, W1W 7DF
www.morplan.com

FURTHER READING

Aldrich, Winifred, *Metric Pattern Cutting*, Harper Collins, 1991

Cloake, Dawn, *Fashion Design on the Stand*, B T Batsford Ltd, 1996

Haggar, Ann, *Pattern Cutting for Lingerie, Beachwear and Leisurewear*, BSP Professional Books, 1990

Holman, Gillian, *Pattern Cutting Made Easy*, B T Batsford Ltd, 1997

Stanley, Helen, *Modelling and Flat Cutting for Fashion*, Hutchinson Education Ltd, 1983

INDEX